D1551150

PRAGUE
in History
of Music

MILAN KUNA & JIŘÍ VŠETEČKA

PRAGUE IN HISTORY OF MUSIC

The dominating heights above the Vltava river, such as the hill of Vítkov, the ancient Vyšehrad citadel emblazoned with legends, the Petřín hill watchtower or the pathway enabling picturesque vistas from the Strahov monastery, the view points from Prague Castle and the footpaths of the Letná plain, the elevation over the Nusle valley or the Barrandov steep rock – all of them provide us with a view of dozens of spires and turrets which gave the city its sobriquet as "the town of a hundred spires". Moreover, the unrivalled charm of Prague consists also in the shape of the Vltava river bed arched over by both modern and ancient bridges. Although complicating natural orientation in the old city quarters the Vltava river provides them with a quite unique compactness. Thanks to this fact, the gemstone of the city, Prague Castle, can be seen from almost every-

where – as a mysterious, fairy-tale symbol of the city embracing in one whole its history from the early Middle Ages up to the present days. Under the many spires we find Gothic and Baroque galleries enticing the visitors to Prague into peerless views of the roofs of the old houses, palaces and their gardens. The remains of the city ramparts are lined here and there with ancient battlements while some of the lanes and squares have preserved their arcades. Although many capitals including Rome, Vienna, Budapest, Paris, Madrid, London or Amsterdam which have played a prominent role in the cultural development of Europe from time immemorial can also boast of the splendour of their churches, cathedrals, theatres, castles, palaces, gardens and other architectonic sights, the city of Prague has preserved an exceptionally honourable status among them. The grandeur of its dominating feature, Prague Castle, is unparalleled in European and worldwide terms. Prague has witnessed both fame and humiliation, pillage and immense bloom, heroic deeds for the protection of the conviction of its

ISBN 80-85894-42-4

PPS

inhabitants and defeats of the mighty, particularly the nobility and the kings – and in spite of this fact it raised its head again to attain its ethnic, religious and cultural peculiarity. It struggled for not being defeated by the encirclement of the not always amicable and sometimes even venomous surrounding world. In this struggle for its existence in the very heart of Europe it eventually became an important intersection of the cultural efforts and a junction of the domestic and foreign influences which stamped it ultimately with a distinctive individuality. Music in connection with architecture, visual arts and with the special charm of the architectonic layout of its quarters turned Prague into a gem of culture and one of the most remarkable and popular cities in Central Europe.

Well, let us take a very brief look at the history of music which is inseparably bound together with Prague, with this residence of the legitimate and forced representatives or inheritors of the Kingdom of Bohemia. Since the time of the original settlements through its urban construction and its development into a modern metropolis this place addressed by the local population as the heart of the homeland and the mother of all Czech towns has been endowed with exquisite musical creativity – both in the field of interpretation and creation, in the sacred and secular spheres, in concerts and theatres, from simple popular music to music comprising a programme of national revival and constitutional law. Here, with the exception of the suburbs damaged by the totalitarian regime, the architectonic styles consort with each other from the Romanesque, Gothic, Renaissance, Baroque and Art Nouveau styles up to the resourceful Modernism. In this city the role of music was irreplaceable and was always putting the finishing touches to its original spiritual atmosphere providing it with the specific features of the cultural life of its residents which is so difficult to define. In the course of all the past centuries, music in Prague has been something which pertains to its very nature and which makes it indeed a cultural and musical city in the best sense of the term.

No thesis, no statement of the type that Bohemia was the conservatoire of Europe or that music is one of the most characteristic expressions of the Czech nation as we can hear from time to time from somebody enthused in euphoria over the achievements of the Czech music can capture the true picture and sense of the musical activity in Prague. Let us keep in mind the fact that this activity consists of small and big deeds more or less original or taken over from elsewhere but now with the finishing touches produced by the extraordinary sense of music of the Czech people, by artistic personalities as well as by the artistic potency of instrumental and vocal ensembles whose qualities and high standard are beyond all doubts. If this book supplemented with pictures of memorable places connected with the musical activities of the Czech nation during the centuries of its development would contribute to a deeper understanding of the musical peculiarities and exemptions of Prague then its purpose would be unquestionably fulfilled.

In the Medieval period

The oldest Slavonic musical expressions whose existence is mentioned in old chronicles and annals have remained unknown for us. In this respect, archaeological findings of musical instruments are of minor help since most of their components were destroyed in the course of time. Although it is possible now and then to produce a sound from some of the bone pipes, primitive trumpets or clay drums these instruments cannot in the least give us an approximate idea of the musical feeling of the then people. Several chroniclers mention "profligate" dance and warrior songs, night time singing of people over the deceased and even "devilish" songs as they called the heathen songs but provide no information about

The Romanesque rotunda of St. Martin in Vyšehrad from the late 11th century is the oldest preserved monument of the then residence of the Přemyslid princes. The Vyšehrad chapter and its school founded under prince Vratislav II (crowned as the king Vratislav I) played a significant role in the promotion of Gregorian chant in Bohemia. The Rotunda can be found near the massive Baroque Leopold Gate

The gems of the city over the Vltava river – Prague Castle and Vyšehrad citadel – connected with the history and the present of Bohemia – the centres of its culture in the ancient past. Music and singing could be heard here for centuries reflecting the time, development standard and current social and political state of the whole country

Sacred songs connected with music were sung in the Romanesque Prague in its monasteries and churches. The Holy Rod rotunda at the corner of the Streets Karoliny Světlé and Konviktská in the Old Town dates back to the early 12th century. It survived even the disfavours of the ages representing a rare evidence of the Romanesque culture in Prague

their character, rhythm and tonal structure. Despite this fact it would be fatuous to thing that the people of the early Middle Ages, be it in Prague or in its surroundings, did not sing and accompany such singing by musical instruments made from the then available materials. These expressions bore the character of a complex art comprising not only musical but also dancing elements and were a part of various rituals aimed at ensuring fertility and good harvest or controlling the processes of nature. Here, however, the stumbling block is the non-existence of musical notation which would help to reconstruct the music of that time. How happy were the Egyptologists who for the sake of understanding sacred literature produced seve-

St. Adalbert, the second bishop of Prague and the Czech patron who died in 997 during his missionary journey was the founder of the first friary in Bohemia – in the Prague district of Břevnov. Already from its establishment in 993, here divine service singing was cultured and thanks to its founder the monastery enjoyed extraordinary favour of the rulers. The today Baroque complex was built in the first half of the 18th century according to the project of Christopher and Kilian Ignaz Dienzenhofer

ral hundreds years before Christ deciphered the unintelligible hieroglyphs, hence enriching the world by a tremendous area of cultural history. The musical history of the early ages is lacking this opportunity of cognizance.

This is also the reason why the account of the music from the beginning of the Czech state in the 10th century under the reign of the Přemyslid dynasty up to the advent of the Luxembourg dynasty in the 14th century is only in the form of a torso. We know that music and singing at that time were a part of the holidays as well as weekdays and such musical events are depicted also in some of the rare manuscripts. But we know only some spheres of music. When the Roman-Latin orientation gain a victory in the church almost all of the documents of the Old Slavonic culture connected with the names of Cyril (Constantine) and Methodius were destroyed. Many irreplaceable rare documents of a number of Medieval presbyteries and monasteries were destroyed in the time of the Hussite reformation in the early 15th century. In addition, it must be noted that only from about the 11th century musical notation started to develop gradually from the so-called no-line neume notation (approximate marking of melodic move) to a more exact choral notation (with line staff and clefs) and finally up to mensural notation (recording exactly not only the pitch but also the duration of the notes).

Prague in the times of the Přemyslid state was the point of intersection of various influences the most important of which was the introduction of the Latin liturgical singing. It was a process that led the una voce Gregorian chant to an absolute victory. Although it went through development and style variations in various parts of Europe its musical form was fixed for long centuries. Like in other countries, in Prague it was not grown from domestic roots but penetrated through missions from Western Europe and particularly from the Frank Empire since the 9th century because the Czech lands were subordinated to the diocese in Regensburg and then also the archdiocese in Mainz. Gregorian chant was gradually adopted and became established in the Czech lands. It became the official liturgical song model which within the all-European framework laid the foundati-

The first Benedictine nunnery was established in the St. George's church in Prague Castle by Mlada, the sister of Boleslav II in 993. The St. George's church with the nunnery were known for the passion plays depicting the scenes near the Christ's grave. It was an exception that their performance was participated also by the nuns. The Prague St. George's nunnery was one of the most significant cultural centres of the Přemyslid Bohemia

The basilica of St. George in Prague Castle is a significant historical and cultural monument of the Přemyslid period of the Czech state. It is famous also for its songbooks in which, beside the liturgical plays and various types of monodic choral, also the oldest records of the medieval polyphony in the Czech lands have been preserved. Even today significant musical bodies have their productions in the basilica – here the ensemble "English Serenata"

ons of the Western musical culture incorporating, in terms of culture, the Czech lands into this geographical context. The important act for its acceptance in Prague was the establishment of the Prague diocese in 973. A significant role in promoting Gregorian chant in Bohemia was played also by the chapter and its school founded about 1070 at Vyšehrad which was the second biggest hill-fort after Prague Castle in the Medieval Prague. The chant was learnt in Prague also by the members of the princely family in the monastery schools. They participated in various non-liturgical ceremonies or events, sang on the occasion of coronations of princes and nominations of bishops, welcoming receptions of rare guests and many other festive events. However, the divine service proper was reserved for the clergy.

The advancement of the Romanesque Prague was accomplished by Vladislav II who for his services to the Emperor was granted royal dignity. In 1140 Vladislav established the Premonstratensian monastery with the Church of Assumption of Our Lady in the district of Strahov in front of Prague Castle. The monastery started to be the centre of knowledge, writing – including collections of musical works – and culturing of divine service singing. Its collection of the musical works, librettos and iconography documents the spiritual and secular development of music in Prague

In almost the whole of Western Europe the most important centres for the production of divine service chant were monasteries and Prague was no exception in this respect. The most important monasteries included the Benedictine nunnery founded in 967 in Prague Castle and the Benedictine monastery in the district of Břevnov established in 993 as well as the Premonstratensian monastery in the district of Strahov founded in 1140. By the 12th century, all of the main types of divine service chants

From its very establishment, the focal point of knowledge in the Gothic time was the Claris nunnery in Prague whose abbess was Agnes Přemyslid (Anežka Přemyslovna), the daughter of Přemysl I Ottokar and sister of Wenceslas I. The activity of this woman was tremendous and her deeds came into legends. The nunnery was established in 1233–1234 by Wenceslas I

had been documented in this environment: songs for the mass with their constant parts Kyrie, Gloria, Credo, Sanctus, Benedictus, Agnus and variable parts, as well as singing of psalms, hymns and antiphonies which formed component parts of the so-called canon hours. Common folk sang the so-called litanies generally during processions in which God was asked for assistance in their painful earthly progress. A new medieval level of chant in which also the beginnings of the Czech musical creativity started to be expressed is represented by the so-called tropes, sequences and hymns.

Moreover, singing of the so-called rhymed offices (which were sets of chants created in honour of significant saints – in the Czech lands

The Old New Synagogue from 1270 reminds of the size and richness of the Jewish community in the medieval Prague. Even in the Jewish part of the Old Town one could hear sung prayers, singing and music. Sometimes they were not merry and lively because the repeated violence during the pogroms was bringing about fear and fright. Lamentable songs could be heard from the Old New Synagogue especially during the most bloody pogrom in 1389. The appalling testimony of those events was recorded by the scholar and poet Avigdor Karo

particularly in honour of St. Ludmilla, St. Prokop and St. Wenceslas) developed in monasteries and cathedrals. In Prague Castle, mainly in the St. George's Convent, the so-called passion plays were performed in which the scenes near the Christ's grave were presented (visiting of the three Marys, revelation of Christ to Mary Magdalene, etc.). Here, as an exception, the performances were participated also by nuns. In the course of time, their topics were extended also to non-biblical scenes – such as scenes in the hell with devils and Lucifer, consultation of the Jews with Pilate as well as funny and satirical episodes. These dramas included both solo singer parts and choir parts, their lyrics were turned into Czech and folk elements predominated over the choral ones. A special form of the Easter

At the corner of the Týnská Lane running to Old Town (Staroměstské) square there is a Gothic house of the Stone Bell (U Kamenného zvonu) which is a valuable architectural monument from the middle of the 13th century. After its reconstruction in the first half of the 14th century it belonged to the most magnificent burgher houses in the Old Town. A guest of its owners often was John of Luxembourg during his visits to Prague. It is sure that also here one could hear the singing of John's chivalrous suite – his secretary was Guillaume de Machaut, one of the greatest composers of his time

drama was the so-called planctus, weeping of Virgin Mary over the cross of Christ. This musical form acquired popularity due to its touching emotionality. All these phenomena made St. George's Convent in Prague one of the most significant cultural centres of the Přemyslid Bohemia. Of exceptional value are the hymnbooks of this convent in which, beside the liturgy plays and various types of monodic plainsongs, also the oldest records of medieval polyphony in the Czech lands have been preserved: these include chant for two voices in free chant rhythmic mode (the so-called organum style).

The Romanesque architectural style which was connected, among other things, with the grandiose development of the Lesser Town be-

Velislav's Bible (National Library XX IIIC 124, facsimile published by Karel Stejskal. In Cimelia Bohemica 1970, Vol. 12) was produced about 1340 to the order of Master Velislav – canon, diplomat and notary of the kings John of Luxembourg and Charles IV. It is the most extensive medieval picture book in Central Europe. The illustrations are drawn in pen and only slightly coloured. The topics are the Old and New Testaments, anti-Christ and legends. Musical instruments from the time of the production of this Bible edition are represented by the picture (fol. 72 r) "Ceremony of Playing Women" led by Mary the Prophet, Moses's and Aaron's sister

low the Castle in connection with the German colonization under the reign of Přemysl Ottokar II (1253–1278) preserved in Prague its full vitality until the half of the 13th century. Prague was a double-city conurbation where both its parts on the left and right Vltava river banks lived side by side in close vicinity and the closest possible communication. Nevertheless, the Gothic style started to assert itself in both the city parts from the half of the 13th century, particularly in new religious buildings, such as the church of the Holy Saviour, the convents of St. Francis and St. Clara, the presbytery of the church of Our Lady Below Chain, etc. In Prague, this transition from one style to another was carried out slowly, spontaneously, always with respect to the overall character of the city. This symbiosis of styles has remained typical of Prague up to the modern age.

In compliance with the development of chant in Christian Europe a reform of church singing took place also in Prague. It was performed by the dean of St. Vitus's chapter whose name was Vitus who arranged not only the construction of a new organ but also the production of new song books for the sake of unifying choral singing. The most precious manuscripts produced at that time in the church environment at Prague Castle include undoubtedly the St. Vitus's chapter tropes book from 1235. Dean Vitus established a choir of the so-called bonifants, i. e. good boys who were selected from the poorest pupils of St. Vitus's school. Soon,

Velislav's Bible (National Library XX IIC 12, facsimile published by Karel Stejskal. In Cimelia Bohemica 1970, Vol. 12). The Lord on the throne (fol. 155 r) in the circle of 24 old men holding in their hands the following musical instruments: fidula, lyre, and tympanum – the trapezoidal instrument. It is a reflection to revelation of St. John: John saw Christ on a throne in front of whom seven links were burning, around him were four creatures similar to lion, bull, man and eagle and around them were 24 old men with gold crowns holding a harp sitting on thrones

St. Vitus's chapel is the central chapel of St. Vitus's cathedral. The argillite statue of St. Wenceslas dates back to 1378 and its author was Henry Parler. At the end of the 12th or the beginning of the 13th century the song calling up the patron of the country "Svatý Václave" ("Holy Wenceslas") was created. Although it is composed of choral elements people accepted it as a symbol of the Czech state sovereignty and expressing the faith in a lasting preservation of the existence of the Czech nation. It was particularly in the period of wars and threat to the country that the song proved its high moral and encouraging power

such choirs of materially ensured singers were established also in Vyšehrad chapter and the Old Town church of St. Gallus. Ennoblement of music in St. Vitus's basilica was contributed also by a costly renovation of the cathedral.

The oldest known song which common people could sing in church in the Czech language was the liturgy hymn "Hospodine, pomiluj ny" which evolved from the original invocation Kyrie Eleison ("Lord, have mercy") from the 11th century. This song played an extraordinary role in the history of the Czech musical culture. It became property of all people, its tune was simple but not primitive, people sang this hymn not only in divine service but also before big battles in order to get God's blessing and protection. The popularity of this song was so big that in the Middle Ages it became the national anthem.

Another significant song from the time of the reign of the Přemyslid princes dates back to the late 12th century and the early 13th century. It is named "Svatý Václave" ("Holy Wenceslas") and is as famous as its predecessor, the hymn addressing God. Although it is composed from choral elements people accepted it as a symbol of the Czech state and trust in a lasting survival of the Czech nation. It was especially in war periods that this song proved its high moral and encouraging power.

In the field of secular musical culture there was a development of chivalry songs, particu-

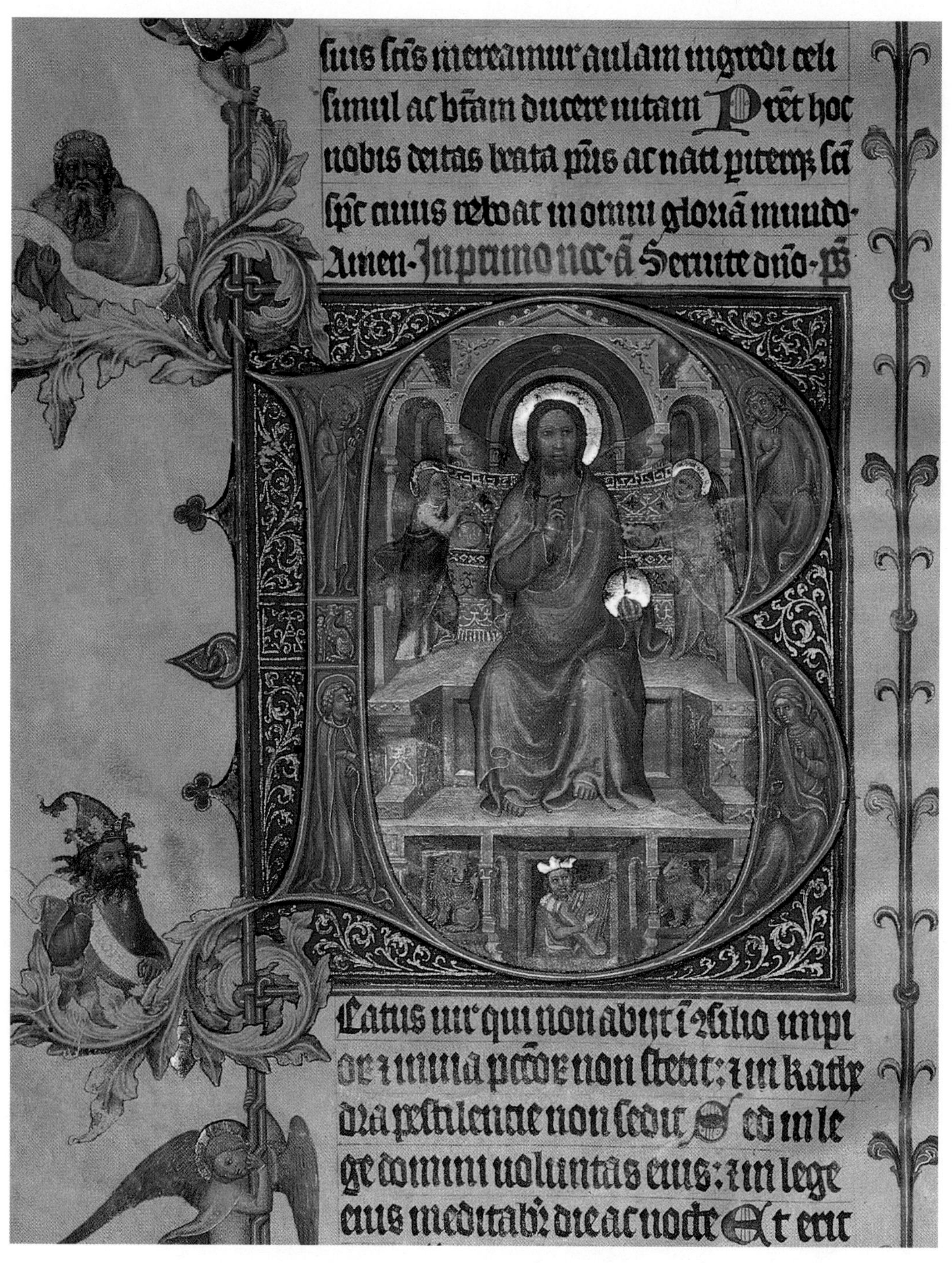

Liber viaticus by John of Středa (National Museum Library XIII A 12) – the bishop and chancellor of Charles IV from the years 1360–1364. The initial shows Christ sitting on the throne and below him is a musician with psaltery. This instrument was popular in the 14th and 15th centuries together with harp. It is a rather shallow resonation chest in the form of trapezium with strings running across it which were thrummed with fingers

Active building bustle could be seen in Vyšehrad under the reign of the Emperor Charles IV, who returned the splendour of a sovereign's castle to the former Přemyslid residence. Vyšehrad underwent a costly reconstruction of the royal palace and the church. The ruler was generous also in relation to the chapter so that the importance of the second castle of Prague increased both politically and as a centre of spiritual life. The religious king also renewed the coronation path of the kings of Bohemia from Vyšehrad to Prague Castle

larly at the courts of the European rulers. At the turn of the 11th century this music was produced by the so-called troubadours in the principalities in South France and by trouveres in North France while in Germany by minnesingers who brought this culture to Prague. This sung lyrics extolled chivalry virtues, such as bravery, loyalty, devoted service of a vassal to his feudal master and his chosen lady. Although it is not excluded that the beginnings of chivalry songs at the Prague princes court date back already to the 12th century, imports of the German artificial song – the so-called minnesang – took place not until the reign of the last Přemyslid kings (1230–1305). At the court of the Přemyslid princes there were always many musicians who were able to move and entertain the audience by their songs and their playing musical instruments. They were real masters of the musical trade. It was not seldom that they were honoured by a virtually "royal" respect. The oldest musicians at the Czech royal court

Liber viaticus by John of Středa (National Museum Library XIII A 12) from the years 1360–1364 belongs to the gems of literature. It contains, among other things, also marvellous illuminations and decorated initials. This initial shows king David with musicians – one of them playing the horn, the other a small drum. David, the king of Israel, was a musician and is considered to be the author of the Book of Psalms

The main temple of the country – St. Vitus's cathedral in Prague Castle – is often the place of ceremonial masses or concerts. Beside the famous Czech musical bodies also a number of world renowned ensembles made their productions in the cathedral – here, the Liverpool Philharmonic Orchestra

PRAŽSKÉ JARO

known by their names were Dobřeta and Kojata, the so-called "jokulators", who performed, among other things, court epics, praised and extolled brave deeds of their ruler and his family. It was not seldom that these singers were granted precious gifts – even yeoman farms. The first known German minnesinger at the court of Wenceslas I whose rule took place from 1230 to 1253, was Reinmar von Zwetter and his successor Meister Sigeher, then Neidhardt von Reuenthal and others. A great number of minnesingers lived also at the court of Přemysl Ottokar II, such as Frederic von Sunburg, Ulrich von Eschenbach and others who accompanied the king of Bohemia also during his war campaigns ensuring his amusement after exhausting battles. On the occasion of the coronation of Wenceslas II in 1297 and during his rule (1283–1305) significant minnesingers and jokulators from the whole of Central Europe came to his court to Prague. Wenceslas II himself was the author of several court songs! When the king died his death was mourned for by songs by Heinrich von Meissen who was called Frauenlob (died 1318), one of the best minnesingers of his time.

Adjacent to the Royal Palace in Prague Castle is the Chapter church of All Saints built in 1370–1387 by Peter Parler. The architectural style was undoubtedly inspired by the Paris St. Chapelle. Charles IV established the college chapter in the church whose members were elected from among the masters of Charles University. Here, a performance of the ensemble Schola Gregoriana Pragensis

Under the rule of the Luxembourg dynasty minnesang still lives also at the court of John Luxembourg. This sovereign who ruled from 1310 to 1346 dwelled only seldom at Prague Castle but his secretary was the French composer Guillaume de Machaut (about 1300–1377), one of the greatest authorities in the field of chivalry songs. In 1323–1340, this exceptionally talented man travelled with his king throughout Europe and came, from time to time, also to Prague. He wrote many celebrating songs in verse in honour of King John. At the same time, Machaut was a foremost representative of music polyphony of Ars nova, the author of motets and cantilena songs extolling love and drawing inspiration from the forms of trouver singing.

In particular, the Emperor Charles IV possessing the Czech throne in 1346–1378 was a ruler who strove to make Prague a glowing reflection of his might worthy of representing his residence. This was also connected with the fact that from 1355 the capital of the Kingdom of Bohemia was also the capital of the Holy Roman Empire which turned it into a significant focal point of a magnificent dynastic policy. When the young ruler who was brought up in France succeeded to the throne after the death of his father John Luxembourg he subordinated to this aim almost all of his activities: he started with reconstruction of the royal palace, achieved promotion of the Prague bishopric to archbishopric, started construction of a new Gothic cathedral at Prague Castle, got built

The Old Town burghers were granted permit by king John of Luxembourg in 1338 to establish their own town hall. The Gothic building of the town hall was accomplished at the end of the 15th century already under the rule of the Jagello dynasty. This musician with a lute has its origin in the medieval period of construction

a stone bridge connecting the Prague Lesser Quarter with the Old Town, founded the district of the Prague New Town and a great number of new monasteries. He had a glorious coronation in Prague which could not do without music. However, music is revived again also straight at Charles's court. The King and Emperor keeps pipers (Svach, Mařík) and buglers (John Velek) and, possibly, a bigger group of musicians. The minnesinger Heinrich von Mügeln was also active here until 1358. Numerous wall paintings and book illuminations from this time inform indirectly about the fact that also instrumental music was performed frequently at the court of the Luxembourg kings in Prague even though its notation records are very rare. Charles IV to-

ok care also for the enhancement of church singing: he established or renewed the St. Vitus chapter choruses (in 1343 he founded the significant and influential chorus of 24 "mansionaries" who continuously provided the singing of canon hours and in 1360 a chorus of 12 psalmists, re-established the bonifants chorus, etc.). Further efforts for a unification of liturgy singing was exercised by the Prague Archbishop Ernest of Pardubice who was in this post in 1344–1364. He arranged the production of new magnificent choral books for the mass and canon hour ceremonies which have been preserved almost completely and in which the specifically Czech branch of choral notation, the so-called nota rhombica (rhombic note) was used.

The most memorial architectural sights of the Old Town of Prague include the Carolinum established by Charles IV. The bay–window university chapel in the south front of the building dates back to the time before 1390. Students and masters of all the Central Europe met in Prague university from 1348. Compulsory disciplines in Charles university included also theoretical study of music

Charles IV himself got inspiration both from Italian Humanism and French culture which expressed itself favourably also in the development of arts in the Prague environment. Under his rule, secular songs, instrumental music and polyphony had the best prerequisites for advancement even though the Catholic clergy took care that this type of songs and music which they ascribed as mere "ear tickling" would not penetrate to the religious environment.

In spite of this, as soon as in the time of Charles IV an institution was founded in Prague which not only played a positive role in educating the cultural class of people and stirred up the surface of the on-coming Reformation but had an influence also on the development of music and its exacting theories. This institution was the Prague university founded in 1348 which was a place of meeting of students and masters from the whole Central Europe and where theoretic study of music belonged to compulsory disciplines. Although music in this time was perceived and studied with respect the Middle Ages – including the ideas prevailing at the Prague university – did not attribute creative abilities to the musicians. This was based on the conviction that if man was created by God also music was a work of God; the capacity of a musician was only to reveal and express it. Therefore, the pictures of St. Gregory in the Prague illuminated books, for instance, suggest the following concept: it was the Holy Spirit who whispered or dictated him Gregorian chant. However, also other contemporary opinions attributed the creation of some songs either to famous saints, e. g. St. Adalbert allegedly is the author of the hymn "Hospodine, pomiluj ny", or to popular reformers, e. g. Master John Huss allegedly created songs, which, however, is inconsistent with historical truth (in fact he made some adaptations of the lyrics of a couple of songs).

The Prague university environment of early Humanism is connected also with the creation of Latin liturgy song called cantio. It was a production in which a considerable role was played by Virgin Mary and Christmas themes and lyrical poetry concerning saints. It often took its tunes also from secular folk songs. Cantio was partly composed also in polyphony. Interest in these songs survived up to the end of the 15th century, especially at the Prague university from which this type of songs spread abroad. Beside this Latin songs and Czech strophic liturgy songs, more artificial liturgy songs of domestic origin, the so-called "leichs" began to be produced in the 14th century. However, the most characteristic of the song production of

Stone bridge, called Charles bridge since 1870, is the oldest communication of Prague connecting the towns bellow Prague Castle. At the Lesser Quarter end it is guarded by two towers while the Old Town end has a massive Bridge Tower, a gem of architecture of the era of Charles IV. On the occasion of Charles coronation as Czech king this was the way of the ceremonial coronation procession from Vyšehrad to Prague Castle. The glorious ceremony could not do without accompaniment of music and signing

the late medieval Prague is the penetration of topical social and often also polemical themes into its contents which indicates already a distinct trend leading to the Hussite revolution.

However, the Prague of the Luxembourg era did not have only hymns and unison songs. A record in a monastery inventory from this time even indicates the existence of a "liber discantorum operis Pragensis", i. e. books of descants created in Prague. This suggests that in the 14th century in Prague (most probably in St. Vitus's Chapel) descants, i. e. mensural polyphonic liturgy compositions could be heard as they started to be produced by the composers of the notre dame school in Paris round 1200. On the other hand, the chronicler Peter Žitavský from Zbraslav monastery near Prague writes about the year 1330 that singing in "broken voices" (i. e. polyphony in fifths and fourths which used to be produced long ago by trained musicians) can be heard today on dancing occasions as well as in squares. This remarkable notice proves that mensural polyphonic motets and songs as they developed from the notre dame initiatives in Europe in the era of ars antiqua started at this time to be extended also both to entertainment events and to musical productions in the streets of the Luxembourg Prague. Who knows whether the extraordinary sense of music of the Czech people which became famous in later centuries had not its foundation already in the Prague of the Luxembourgs?

The Grim Reaper and Passion, two coloured wooden figures to the right of the astronomical dial of the Old Town hall clock. Passion holds a musical instrument in one hand which is here the symbol of connection of the worldly delights linked with music while the Grim Reaper represents the inevitable end. The figures (a total of 8 by the sides of the astronomical and calendar dial) date back to the 18th century. The astronomical clock was built in the Old Town hall in the 15th century

We have suggested already that the church was adverse to an active singing participation of common people in the divine service. Despite this fact it did not manage to prevent some songs to assert themselves in singing of the people in church or temple. Their lyrics were Czech, understandable and popular with all people. This kind of famous songs which maintained their priority up to the Hussite period included, for instance, the celebrating song "Buoh všemohúcí" ("Almighty God") and the song "Jezu Kriste, štědrý kněže" ("Jesus Christ, Generous Prince"), an excellent example of European spiritual lyrical poetry as such. When the priest of the Prague church of Our Lady Before Týn tried to forbid the people to sing the former song this raised such a turmoil in the city that even the Prague Archbishop Olbram had to intervene in favour of the song and put the poor priest in jail. The latter song then became a part of the basic song repertoire of Bohemian Brethren and passed even to the song collections of the German Reformation. When in 1408 the Prague synod dealt with the problem of liturgy songs which could and which could not be permitted to the people it arrived positively only at four songs – those most famous – "Hospodine, pomiluj ny", "Svatý Václave", "Buoh všemohúcí" and "Jezu Kriste, štědrý kněže". Despite this fact we cannot say that the orders of the synod have been ever fulfilled consistently. The Czech people coming closer to an outburst in the revolutionary Hussite movement were no more willing to reconcile themselves with their being curbed so severely in their rights. Their own creativity, likeness for sacred song and moral values represented by these song gems were more precious and more sacred for the people than the orders of the clergy which were held more and more evidently in contempt by common people and the burgher estate in Prague.

In the Hussite period

It is difficult to separate the development of music in the Hussite period in Prague from the development of music in the whole territory of Bohemia. The focal point of musical activities and musical forms shifted to different areas than was the case elsewhere in the world. It is still a question whether this situation by which Prague differed from the rest of Europe was a contribution or, to the contrary, a retarding element.

More important was that under the influence of the Hussite preachers who criticized abuses in society and pointed out the demoralization of the current Catholic clergy it was the sacred song that expressed a new view of the world: it even became an expression of a new ideology. Radical Hussites – both in the country and in Prague – refused Latin and put Czech elements into the services. They were convinced that common people should understand these rites and take an active part in them. Accordingly, even Gregorian chant was sung in Czech. Unlike works of visual arts which were removed from churches by the Hussites the new sacred song became the most natural expression of the folk feeling and thinking. In particular, numerous tunes and songs responding to the sweeping events of the time appeared among the people after the speeches of the Hussite preachers. This was also the case of the Bethlehem chapel in the Old Town of Prague which was the first Hussite temple for three thou-

Master John Huss had sermons in the Bethlehem chapel regularly in 1402–1412. His audience sung spiritual songs in Czech before the sermon. Many of these songs spread fast throughout Prague and the whole Bohemia thanks to their attractive melodies which were easy to remember. Also today the renewed space of the chapel serves as a place of festive concerts and meetings. In this case it is the inauguration of the rector and deans of the departments of the Czech University of Technology

The Bethlehem chapel in the Old Town of Prague was established by the patricians Kříž and Hanuš of Mühlheim at the end of the 14th century. At that time it was a place were sermons were held in Czech and spiritual songs were sung in Czech by the participants to the service. Its history is connected closely with the names of the significant religious reformers – John Huss and James of Stříbro who worked here at the beginning of the 15th century

sand believers. Its layout disposition, simplicity and plainness of the interior room corresponded with the Reformation religious feeling. Here, Master John Huss (about 1369–1415) preached sermons in the years 1402–1412 and by his fearless ideas of God's truth and the necessity of a change of the clerical practices he stirred up enthusiasm in common people. Before the sermon – in the Bethlehem chapel and in other Hussite churches – the Prague people sung their older and new songs and in some of them they even added new strophes, for instance in the song "Svatý Václave". Its up-to-dated verses called up this patron of Bohemia "not to let die us nor the future ones" and in this optimistic spirit the song produced its effect on the Czech people for long centuries. Many of these songs spread throughout Prague and Bohemia by means of leaflets but, chiefly, thanks to their attractive melodies which were easy to remember. One of the first of such Hussite songs was "Slyšte, rytieři boží" ("Hear, God's Knights") focused against the Archbishop Zbyněk Zajíc of Hasenburg. When Master John Huss was burnt at the stake in Constance on 6 July, 1415 the Hussites accused the enemies of "their" Master also by a song – "O svolánie konstantské" ("The Council of Constance") composed on a general tune. Before this, however, the so-called Praguers – the followers of Huss who symbolically took communion from chalice – responded in November 1415 to the burning of Huss by attacking presbyteries and churches and forced

The Old Town church of St. Martin in the Wall in Martinská Street is significant for the history of the Hussite movement. Here, in the autumn 1414, upon initiative of John Huss's friend James of Stříbro also the laic public was given the Calixtine-type host and wine. Songs were sung here in Latin and Czech in the Hussite period. From the musical history the church is known for Francis Xaver Brixi, the author of great oratorios, organ player and director of St. Vitus's cathedral who was baptised here in 1732

the malevolent and discredited Holy Roman Emperor and Hungarian King Sigismund to give them permit of taking communion from chalice in eight Prague churches. A revolutionary novelty in the Bethlehem chapel was not only the singing of Czech sacred songs but also the divine service performed since 1417 in the Czech language upon initiative of the followers of the Hussite preacher Jakoubek of Stříbro.

Information about what was sung in the Hussite period and what songs existed for the divine service rites is given most completely by the so-called Jistebnice Hymn Book found in 1872 in the presbytery in Jistebnice near the town of Tábor which today is carefully held in the Prague National Library. Radical Hussites called the Taborites turned the mass rite into Czech and restricted singing only to songs while the Hussite rightists in Prague maintained the Latin rite. The centrist Hussites concentrated around John Želivský used Czechicized hymns, too (their translation into Czech was maybe participated by the Hussite priest John Čapek) as well as the originally Latin lyrics of the mass choral songs and a part of the hour canons, the so-called offices. The Jistebnice Hymn Book is an evidence that Gregorian chant sung in Czech preceded by one century similar efforts in Lutheran Germany.

In Prague, the polyphonic singing with accompaniment of organ, string and woodwind instruments has never been eradicated even in the

"Ktož jsú boží bojovníci" ("Who Are the God's Fighters") (Jistebnice Hymn Book, National Museum Library in Prague) from the early 1420s is the best known Hussite song. It was sung by the Hussite army before the beginning of the struggle. The commandments for the activities of the individual army types – the God's fighters – forms a kind of brief military rules in the text of the song and, therefore, the authorship of the song is ascribed to someone from the vicinity of John Žižka of Trocnov

time of the most severe clashes of the Hussite fighters with the crusade armies. This production of polyphonic music was not free of difficulties because hard criticism from the part of the radical Hussites caused that everything deviating from the character of a folk sacred song was regarded as "saucy tickling and amusing fiddling". It was only thanks to the Praguers that polyphonic sacred singing remained in limited scope in the Hussite repertoire up to the end of this revolutionary period.

Nevertheless, the most precious fruit of Hussite creativity are the warrior songs. They grew from the adamantine faith in God's truth. They were created in fierce fights with the enemies when the people with maces, nailed flails and halberds in hands using brilliantly carriage barriers became the terror of all foreign intruders and local enemies. The Hussite people strengthened their faith by warrior songs of the type of "Slyšte, rytieři boží" or "Povstaň, povstaň, veliké město pražské" ("Rise, Rise, Great City of Prague"). The latter song was even focused against the hated King Sigismund who ruled in Prague after a short episode in 1420 only in the years 1435 to 1437. The victorious Hussite troops were usually welcomed by the local people by exultant singing of the song "Dietky, v hromadu se senděme" ("Children, Let's Come Together").

However, the most famous product of the Hussite revolt was the sacred song "Ktož jsú boží bojovníci" ("Who Are the God's Fighters"). As we perceive it today, the song seems to petrify the glory and heroism of the Czech nation, the trust in God's truth and the desire for life according to the Bible. It is said that the singing of this song raised such a horror in the crusade troops that the enemy forces turned to retreat. The song "Ktož jsú boží bojovníci" was re-discovered by the national revivalists in the 19th century and became the musical symbol of resistance and bravery of the Czech nation as such.

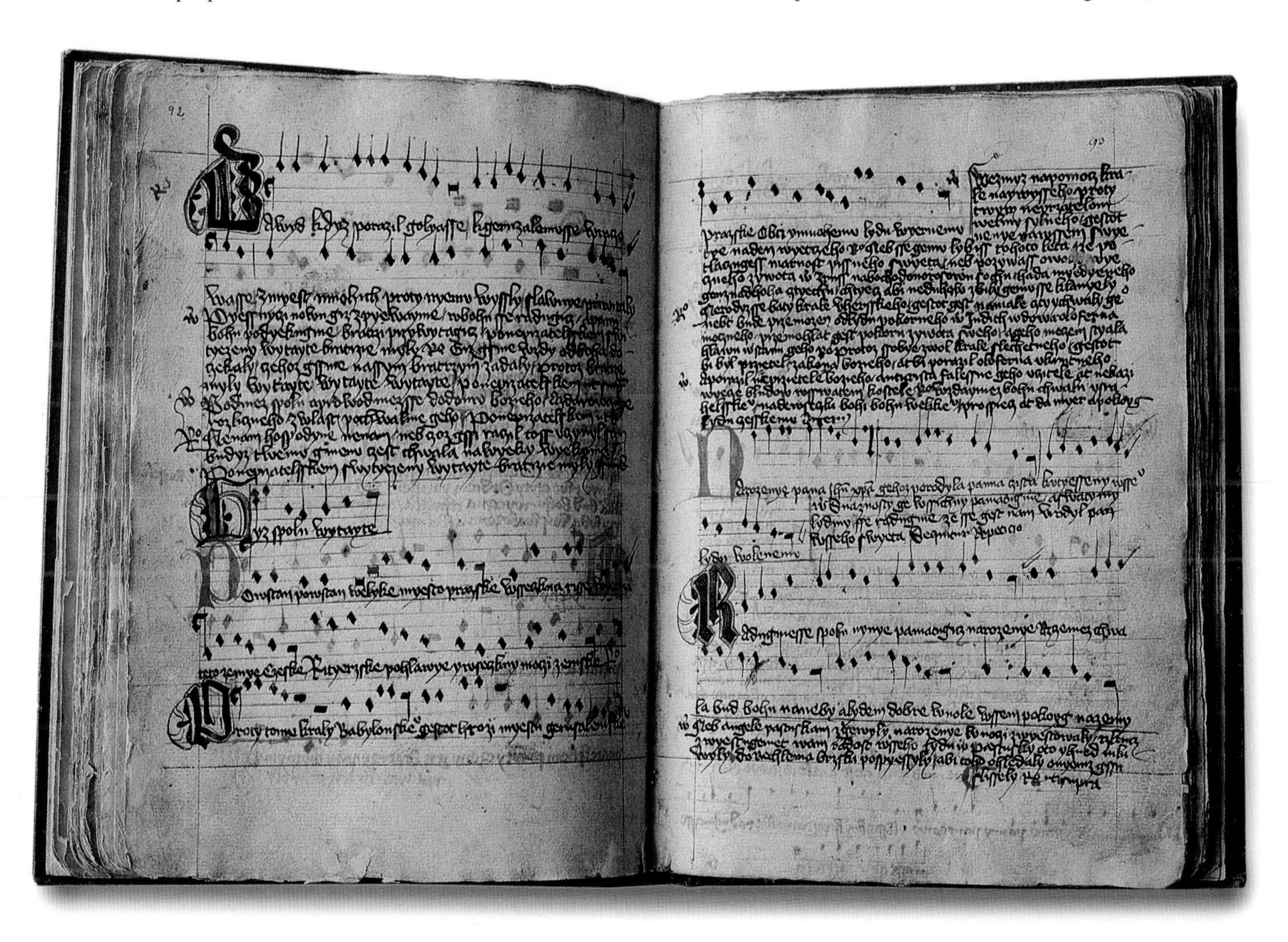

The high altar piece of the Gothic cathedral of Our Lady of the Snow in the New Town is only a part of the originally planned building from the period of Charles IV. In the time of the excited atmosphere of the first half of 1419 it was the place of work of the radical Hussite priest John of Želiv. In that time of extreme religious clashes songs could be heard not only in the cathedrals but polemical religious songs were sung also in the streets of Prague in frequent non-permitted processions of the Calixtine followers

The Jistebnice Hymn Book (National Museum Library in Prague) contains a record of the Hussite song "Povstaň, povstaň, veliké město pražské" ("Rise, Rise, Great City of Prague") which was created during the spring of 1420 when the Hussite Prague intended to defend against the armies of the crusade expedition of the Hungarian and Roman king Sigismund. Its authorship is sometimes attributed to the Hussite priest John Čapek

In the period of Reformation

The Renaissance, Humanism, Reformation – these terms can be attributed to the cultural life of the 15th and 16th centuries almost anywhere in Europe. At the same time they inform us about the fact that this was a period when life was going through surprising and sometimes even never-thought-of changes. In particular, a new type of polyphonic composition was developed in the Netherlands which influenced for a long time the development of arts in the whole of the continent. Characteristic of the new style which was a sort of the opposite pole of the medieval polyphony was a music imitation technique, the levelling of the interlacing voices, respect to harmony of new accords, etc. Only thoroughly trained musicians could master this art. The new way of music creation was applied in the composing of new masses and motets as well as in a whole range of other musical forms.

In the Czech lands, however, the development of music took rather different paths. On the one hand, in the field of artificial polyphony it lagged behind the art grown at the European aristocratic courts and, on the other hand, in the field of sacred singing it overtook Europe by a whole century. After the Hussite revolution particularly the cities represented centres which made the path for the Reformation culture. The power and massiveness of this Reformation endeavour headed by Bohemian Brethren restrained the development of the Renaissance culture in the Czech lands.

The church of Our Lady before Týn whose huge front gable was finished under George of Poděbrady. It used to hold the statue of this ruler and a golden chalice. The church was the main Calixtine temple of the city and sacred songs were sung here but the lead at that time started to be taken over by the Unity of Bohemian Brethren (Unitas Fratrum). The two tall spires of the temple saw the Old Town square when in 1621 the famous Renaissance composer, musician, scholar and traveller, soldier and diplomat Christopher Harant of Polžice was executed here as one of the foremost participants of the Czech estates uprising

Gun tower called Daliborka was finished in 1496 over the moat of Prague Castle in the north-east bending of the rampart wall. The fortification works by the end of the 15th century should ensure the Castle against the efficient range of the improved fire arms. A prison used to be in the ground floor of the tower. The first significant involuntary guest was the knight Dalibor of Kozojedy who, as the legend says, learnt here to play the violin during the long time of his imprisonment. The legend served also as the topic for the opera Dalibor by Bedřich Smetana

Although the first Jesuit college the mission of which was to retain the Reformation ideas in Bohemia, extirpate Utraquists and establish new conditions in the Roman-Catholic spirit, was founded in Prague in 1556 and its residence was in the Prague Clementinum, anti-Reformation was not able to win a more significant recognition until after the defeat of the anti-Hapsburg uprising in the battle of the White Mountain (1620).

Characteristic of the Reformation period in Prague and other Czech cities is the establishing of the so-called brotherhoods of men of letters. These were institutions within the city controlled by the local guild order the core of which consisted of educated burghers, the so-called men of letters. However, they could be joined also by singers and musicians from among craftsmen. The key role in them was played by the wealthy and influential personalities of individual cities. The brotherhoods of men of letters saw their mission in singing during divine services, processions and funerals and on some other social events. With regard to artistic level, there were big differences among them which was dependent not only on their size (from eight people up to big ensembles) but also on the artistic abilities of those who controlled them. Beside monodic hymns, these brotherhoods performed polyphonic music, too. In particular, in large churches during various festivals the brotherhood choirs performed exacting polyphonic singing, the so-called "figural" singing where individual voices often were melodically orna-

The advent of the Hapsburg dynasty to the Czech throne in 1526 started a gradual development of court music. It is sure to be heard also in the rooms of the Royal Belvedere in the time of Ferdinand I. His son the Archduke Ferdinand of Tyrol who represented the ruler in Prague created here a Renaissance court and an independent orchestra and its popularity only strengthened the presentiment of the Prague citizens for this disobedient Hapsburg prince and his beautiful wife Philipina

mented, “figured”, with high demands on the singing technique. According to the repertoire it can be assumed that the brotherhoods of men of letters in Prague reached a high reproduction standard and mediated the exacting art of polyphony to a wide range of audience, which was a valuable work. They livened up their singing productions by playing the organ and other musical instruments. The first brotherhood in the Czech lands was active in Prague in 1439 and then in the course of the 16th century such associations were founded in almost all cities of Bohemia and Moravia. Only big, significant brotherhoods many of which were in Prague acquired for their purposes hymn books with costly decoration according to which their members standing around the pulpit with an open hymn book in front of them performed their musical productions.

One of the most distinctive fields of the Czech music even in European terms was sacred song. The prerequisites for its bloom were created a hundred years ago in the neighbouring Germany by the Hussite movement the heritage of which was resumed by the Czech post-Hussite Reformation in its sacred song. It was no uniform stream because various religious groups tried to differ from and compete with each other with their repertoires but it was singing which curbed the supremacy of Gregorian chant and Latin songs in the church. In contrast to folk songs, these songs were created by Reformation priests and schoolmasters, devout burghers, students, village chro-

The famous “singing fountain” in front of the Royal Belvedere was cast in bronze in 1564–1568 by Thomas Jaroš. The drawing for the fountain was made by the court painter Francesco Terzio and its sculptural work was made by Antonio Brocco. It was named after the sound of the water drops which when falling down on the lower basin of the fountain resemble singing

In the north wing of the 2nd courtyard of the Castle there are Renaissance stables on both sides of the passage through the Powder Bridge. These rooms were adapted at the turn of the 16th and 17th centuries for the housing of Rudolph's Spanish horses. Today the former Imperial stables are used for performances and concerts of musical ensembles

niclers and frequently also contemporary writers. The tunes were often taken over from popular melodies of that time and, partly, new ones were created. Even though the artistic value of these songs can be assessed in different ways their purpose was to promote Christian dogmatics and dissemination of the Gospel ideas as the basis of moral values of a Christian. This is where the power of these songs consisted in. The invention of book-printing brought about the production of collections of these songs called hymn books with thousands of lyrics and melodies. The Reformation's first printed hymn book in Europe was published without notation in Prague in 1501. Due to this, by publishing hymn books with notation of tunes or only with texts which were sung

also by the so-called general tune, a massive spreading of this song treasury was achieved.

The most beautiful and most significant European hymn books of the Reformation period can be found in the Unity of Bohemian Brethren (Unitas Fratrum) who devoted extraordinary attention to the editing work on the songs contained in the hymn books. The first preserved Czech hymn book with notation is the big Bohemian Brethren hymn book edited by John Roh and published in Prague in 1541. Many significant hymn books were printed outside Prague which meant that these collections would not find good application in Prague. The most important and most influential edition of a Bohemian Brethren hymn book was created by the Bohemian Brethren bishop John Blahoslav (1523–1571).

In the north arm of the transept of St. Vitus's cathedral in Prague Castle there is an organ loft produced by Bonifac Wohlmut in 1559–1561. In the loft is Rococo-decorated organ from 1762–1763 from the workshop of the Tachov organ builder Anthony Gartner. Below the loft is the choir chapel of St. Vitus's chapter with net rib vault

The marvellous Spanish hall is one of the most representative rooms of Prague Castle. It is a place of ceremonial social events and today also of significant musical performances – here it is a show of the winners of the radio competition Concerto Bohemia

While people believing sincerely in the possibility of reformation of the church were engaged in musical activities in the framework of the brotherhoods of men of letters, Prague in the Renaissance period – though not to such a degree as elsewhere in Europe – cultured, among other things, also "its" court art. The main centre for this was Prague Castle. In the period of 1458 to 1526 which is the period from the ascending to the throne by the Czech King George of Poděbrady up to the end of the reign of Louis Jagello, the beginnings of this art were modest and we know only about a group of buglers who livened up with their playing the festive events at the court. Not until the ascending of the Hapsburgs to the Czech throne in 1526 the advancement of court music started to develop gradually. Ferdinand I (his reign dates from 1526 to 1564) renewed immediately at his inauguration in Vienna the Hapsburg orchestra which was able to interpret the most demanding musical compositions and which occasionally travelled from Vienna to Prague. However, it had no significant influence on the musical life in the Prague court environment. Moreover, in 1548–1567 there was an independent orchestra of the Archduke Ferdinand who was the son of the Czech king of the same name and intended also in this field to level with the art of the Emperor's court. After nineteen years in Prague, however, the orchestra moved along with

Vast construction adaptations took place in Prague Castle at the turn of the 16th and 17th centuries under the rule of Rudolph II. The remarkable Spanish hall built over the stables of the sovereign's valuable Spanish horses was adapted to the present appearance in the Classicist and Neo-Baroque styles in the 18th and 19th centuries

the Archduke to Innsbruck in the Alps. It was not until the reign of Rudolph II (1576–1611) that the imperial Hapsburg orchestra moved from Vienna to Prague Castle. This settlement of the orchestra in Prague took place in 1583. But under the rule of King Matthias (1611–1619) the orchestra moved back to Vienna. This time it was for good. In this connection it is necessary to mention that several remarkable orchestras of the Czech nobility of the second half of the 16th century were located also outside Prague, for instance the bishopric orchestra in Olomouc and Kroměříž, the Rožmberk orchestra in Český Krumlov and Třeboň. Their inventories give extraordinarily important testimony of the overall standard of this musical culture in the Czech lands.

We must not be confused by the name "court orchestra" in understanding the mission that such musical ensemble had in Rudolph's time. Its members comprised not only instrumental musici-

ans but also singers who provided music during divine services both in the St. Vitus's cathedral and the chapter church of All Saints in Prague Castle. Its core was formed by men and boys choir with a conductor and an organist. In the course of time, however, this orchestra took still more and more substantial part also in non-church events, played in festivals and banquets, welcomed the visitors to the royal court, etc. The extending of this mission at Prague Castle meant that the orchestra was enriched gradually by further musical instruments. In particular, the brass ones – trombones and trumpets – put a polish on its musical productions at especially festive occasions. From the original thirty members the orchestra grew to seventy or more members so that both by the number of musicians and the artistic standard it became one of the foremost musical ensembles of the then Europe. There were mostly foreigners among their members (the Dutch, Italians, Germans, Spaniards) which caused that although the orchestra had a substantial influence on the development of the Czech music in the reproduction sense its influence was lesser in the creative production of new musical values stemming from the domestic resources or those produced by Czech personages of music.

The Reformation period is characterized by the establishing of the so-called brotherhoods of men of letters. Significant brotherhoods, many of which worked in Prague acquired elaborately decorated hymn books and performed their musical productions using them. The Czech Lesser Quarter Gradual from 1569–1572 (National Library XVII A 3, fol. 363 r) contains also this illumination which commemorates the burning of Master John Huss at the stake in Constance and the lyrics of the song in his memory

The church of the Holy Saviour in Salvátorská Street was built in 1611–1614 in the Gothic-Renaissance style for the German Lutherans living in Prague. After the defeat at the White Mountain it was allocated to the order of St. Paul hermits and adapted in Baroque style. Today it is an evangelical church used again for sacred singing and frequent concerts – here the Archi di Praga orchestra

Under the rule of Rudolph II when the court orchestra reached its prime the key role in Prague was played by the best composers of the then Europe. For thirty years it was headed by one of the leading personalities of the high Renaissance – the composer Phillipp de Monte (1521–1603) who composed during his life about one and a half thousand madrigals and who in his time was regarded as "musicorum hoc nostro saeculo princeps", the first musician of the century. He was recommended to Prague by the world-known French-Flemish Renaissance composer Orlando di Lasso (1532–1594) whose works formed a permanent component of the repertoire of the Rudolph's orchestra. Monte's deputy in the orchestra was a similarly excellent Dutch musician Jacob Regnart (about 1540–1599) who after almost twenty years of tireless work in the orchestra died in Prague. We cannot omit the Emperor's organist Charles Luython (1557–1620) who after the death of Monte bore the honorary title of the imperial court composer. Beside these composers and musicians, the excellent singer F. Sales (died 1599) was active in the orchestra as a composer, too.

Over the years of its existence this ensemble had at its disposal an extensive repertoire representing undoubtedly the best works that could be rendered by the famous European composers. The orchestra performed also the works of the Czech aristocrat and significant author Christopher Harant of Polžice and Bezdružice (born 1564) who, unfortunately, was executed at the Old Town square on 21 June, 1621 for his participation in the anti-Hapsburg uprising. Although this courtier, traveller, diplomat and warrior observed the activities of the imperial orchestra only marginally from aside he was excellent at his professionalism particularly in the field of polyphony. What a pity that the life destiny of the Slovenian composer Jacob Gallus-Handl (1550–1591) was not favourable for his more extensive assertion in the Rudolph's orchestra in Prague. Although he ranked among the foremost artists he influenced the musical situation only in monasteries and bishopric residences of smaller towns – mainly in Moravia, Silesia and in Lower Austria. He came to Prague only six years before the end of his relatively short life when he was the organist in the church of St. John. His compositions, however, were known even in the imperial court orchestra with the musicians of which he was in touch frequently. He had close contacts also with the Prague Jesuits which contributed to the spreading of his works within the framework of the anti-Reformation movement. At the end of his life Jacob Gallus-Handl finished and published in Prague, among other things, a four-volume cycle of 374 motets for all the holidays of the church year Opus musicum and three volumes of Latin madrigals for four voices Moralia which belong to the best vocal works of the European Renaissance.

Although at a lower artistic level, of importance for Prague and its musical activities were ensembles of buglers and trombonists. Initially, in Prague and in other Czech cities they performed also other functions (such as security guard and night watchmen) but in the course of time they associated in exclusively musical ensembles. As soon as from 1548 festive tunes were played by the Prague trombone group from the gallery of St. Vitus's Cathedral and after this model a similar group was established by the Old Town of Prague three years later. These musicians played regularly from the church or town hall towers, were helpful on Sundays in the choir, and in the function of the city orchestra they made some money in weddings, fairs and public festivals, on official occasions in town halls, etc. As evidenced by their repertoire they did not make do with a simple playing of some melody with accompaniment but interpreted even deman-

The view from the church of Our Lady before Týn offers a complex of the Town Hall building with a huge tower from the 14th century. To the right is the Baroque church of St. Nicholas from 1732–1735, and in forefront is the Art Nouveau memorial of John Huss from the early 20th century

ding polyphonic works. From the half of the 16th century the speciality of Prague was the existence of a Jewish orchestra which – due to its excellent standard – was often invited to musical productions even outside Prague.

A small association – the Collegium musicum was established in Prague in 1616. This ensemble of about eight burghers performed mainly polyphonic singing. Mostly, its members were educated people who liked to discuss arts and music. It was an ensemble of a characteristic Renaissance style.

Yet to make the picture of the musical Prague of the Renaissance period more complete we must not forget to mention the so-called wandering musicians which were countless in this city and many of which, despite their being poor, belonged to excellent improvisers when playing their instruments. They played for dancing and amusement, in the streets and in pubs and were often hired for private events of the burghers. These musicians included pipers, drummers, buglers, the lute, harp, zither, bag-pipe and portable organ players, etc. Their influence on the overall musical spirit of the city was substantial even though it cannot be overestimated. They formed an integral part of any conurbation including that of Prague. They were real masters of dance music and, in particular, secular town and country folk song which could not be heard in the church, monasteries or at the court but which, beside the Reformation sacred songs, pertained to the crucial treasury of the Czech musical creative work.

In the second half of the 16th century, the Old Town trombonists played from the Town Hall tower for fun of the burghers. The Old Town square witnessed a horrible scene on 21 June, 1621 when the Hapsburg winner put a bloody end to the leaders of the Czech uprising. Ten aristocrats and 17 burghers – fifteen of them from Prague – lost their lives on the installed scuffold

In the period of Baroque

The Loretta complex in the district of Hradčany. The whole complex including the church of the Birth of the Lord was accomplished in the first third of the 18th century around a copy of the Holy House from the Italian Loretta built by the Italian architect Giovanni Battista Orsi in 1626–1627 according to the projects of the architects Christopher and Kilian Ignaz Dienzenhofer. The front spire holds the famous chimes of Virgin Mary created by the clock maker Peter Naumann in 1694

The epoch of the musical Baroque in the Czech lands can be ranged generally by the years 1620 and 1740, i. e. from the defeat of the Czech anti-Hapsburg uprising at the beginning of the Thirty Years' War to the end of the reign of the Emperor Charles VI. In the field of music this period is characterized by entirely different style means than in the period of the Renaissance and Reformation. This is a turning point of crucial importance. One of the pillars of the new style was monody, una voce solo singing accompanied by one instrument or a group of instruments and controlled by harmony feeling close to that of the people of today. In the field of opera, great aria da capo was developed gradually with themes of song and dance character, with advanced coloratura and concertant use of musical instruments. From another point of view this was a period of thorough-bass which became an important means of the vertical manner of musical thinking. Despite this fact, even the advanced polyphonic, counterpoint art in this epoch loses none of its artistic ground. Music of the Baroque includes a number of personalities of diverse style expression from Claudio Monteverdi (1567–1643), through Jean-Baptist Lully (1632–1687) up to Antonio Vivaldi (1678–1741), Johann Sebstian Bach (1685–1750) and Georg Friedrich Händel (1685–1759). The development of concertant compositions of varied instrumental constellations was contributed also by new or improved musical instruments, such as French horns, recorders, transverse flutes of various sizes and colours, oboes and fagots, trombones and high trumpets called clarinoes, and in the ensemble music there was a significant transition from violas to violins as the leading string instrument.

The defeat of the troops of the estates in the battle of the While Mountain in 1620 which enabled the Hapsburgs to reign over the lands of the Czech crown and the subsequent Thirty Years War which brought immense suffering to the population of these lands caused that the Czech music had a hard way to the new musical expression. Military campaigns with all their cruelty, fires of cities and looting, famines connected with epidemics, confiscation of property of the anti-Hapsburg rebels – all these things led to a temporary break of the continuity of the artistic development not only in Prague but in the Czech lands at all. The Catholic church won a monopoly

The Czernin Palace in the district of Hradčany belongs to Prague's High Baroque architecture. Since its establishment in the second half of the 17th century the palace was adapted several times in the following centuries. Of remarkable value is the front producing a monumentally articulated mass opening to Loretánské square in the direction to Prague Castle. Domestic orchestra of Count Czernin played in its salons and the palace garden for the audience as well as dancing events

position and treated people with ruthlessness following from the logic of its dogmas. The service rites of evangelic churches were deemed as heresy, the Czech language in the divine services was restricted, instead of the Reformation singing people were forced to sing anti-Reformation songs promoted by Catholic orders and their clergy. Members of the Czech educated class who did not want to reconcile themselves with the Catholic ideology hegemony in the country, including John Amos Comenius (1592–1670), had to leave their homeland. All this led also in Prague to the fact that the vivid cultural life in Prague Castle characteristic, in particular, of the rule of Rudolph II discontinued since under the rule of Ferdinand II in 1618–1637 the imperial court settled for good in Vienna. Prague the population of which dropped down by one-third to mere 40 thousand people turned into a provincial town.

The Loretta rooms have been connected with musical productions already from the early 18th century. Here, a stable ensemble of musicians was active. The then directors of choir included also Christopher Charles Gayer (died in 1734), one of the founders of the St. Vitus's musical collection. Even here valuable musical materials from the 18th and 19th centuries have been preserved – e.g. the inheritance of John Joseph Strobach, violinist and choir-leader

The main bearers of musical activities in the Prague of the period after the defeat at the White Mountain became the musicians of the city churches. They had their firm salaries and opportunity to make some additional money. The choir directors and organists of parish churches were honoured as respectable citizens and managed to become burghers, i. e. to posses a house. The highest aim in this field, however, was deemed to be the post of a conductor or organist in Prague cathedrals. Despite this fact even these high prestige musician posts were not entirely free from other obligations: for instance, the organ players of the large chapter cathedrals (such as St. Vitus's cathedral) carried out, at the same time, the functions of administrative clerks. In monasteries, music was cultured by priests while in the Jesuit and Piarist colleges by the members of the orders along with their students. Piarists (devoted to pedagogical activities) who unlike Jesuits did not strive to seize positions of power belonged to fervent

The main hall of the abbot prelate residence of the Benedictine monastery in Břevnov was projected in 1716–1721 by the architects Christopher and Kilian Ignaz Dienzenhofer. It is called Theresian Hall in honour of the visit of Maria Theresa and Francis of Lothringen in 1753 with the famous ceiling fresco The Miracle of the Blessed Vintíř. Here is a performance of the famous children choir Bambini di Praga

producers of musical art in Prague and other Czech cities. Intensive music production can be attributed also to the Minorite order. They conferred the title of magister musicae to their members who had merits in the field of music. Such a title pertained, for instance, to Matthew Bohuslav Černohorský whose significance for the Czech music will be mentioned later.

Honoured musicians in this period also were buglers and trombonists in the city ensembles and in military garrisons. They had an estate-based pride and felt superior to the musicians who as serfs were in the services of aristocracy. Such musicians not only served their masters as butlers, valets, servants or modest liveried clerks but their playing in the orchestra was considered to be a part of their overall obligations and they had to play always when the nobility wanted to have amusement at a banquet or dancing.

The interesting sign of three violins on the facade of the house No. 210 in Nerudova Street reminds us of the musical history of the house. The house "U Tří housliček" ("Three Little Violins") was owned in 1667–1748 by three families of Prague violin makers one of whom was the internationally known representative of the Prague violin-maker school Thomas Edlinger

It was not until the economic and political recovery of the new military aristocracy which initially had no understanding for culture that they appropriated also music as a part of their representation. Playing of orchestras could be heard in Prague palaces several of which rank among the top Baroque architectural art (Czernin Palace in the district of Hradčany, the palaces of the families of Nosticz, Lobkowicz, Colloredo, Clam-Gallas, etc.) to put a polish on the social life of the nobility. The 18th century, in particular, was rich in their existence. The most significant orchestras in Prague included those of Prince William Auersperg, Count Louis Joseph Hartig, Count Leopold Ferdinand Kinský, Prince Mannsfeld, Prince Martinicz, Count John Ernest Schaffgotsch, Count Francis Anthony Sporck, Count Christopher Vratislav of Mitrovice and others several of which existed continuously for thirty or more years.

Nevertheless, the natural way of feeling and thinking of common people was represented, in particular, by folk

The vista through Nerudova Street to the cathedral of St. Nicholas which used to contain a Jesuit college. Churches and monasteries belonged in the 17th and 18th centuries to the main centres of cathedral music and the biggest of them had also their own musical bodies. The popular form of the Baroque musical culture was the so-called school theatre which was produced in the Jesuit and Piarist colleges in Prague

song. In the Baroque time it was alive in the country and in Prague. It could be heard at weddings and banquets, dance events and fairs and to a certain degree it influenced the appearance and character of the advanced musical art, especially its rhythmic and melodic aspects. A supplement to folk songs was stall-keeper song which through its epic stories informed about events that happened elsewhere.

The musical Baroque includes also the Reformation sacred song the application of which documents best the time in which it now lived or only struggled along. After the battle of the White Mountain it instantly became an undesired product and moved either to intimate privacy, or to emigration (collections of Reformation songs continued to be published abroad and were secretly transported to Prague). Jesuits who were often unsuccessful in their effort to extinguish in Prague and Bohemia “that Reformation tumour” inherited from the Hussite time chose

The book by John Joseph Božan “Slavíček rájský” (“The Nightingale of Paradise”) (National Library 54 A 36) was printed in 1719. Due to its external appearance it is a representative and extensive printed hymn book. This example is the beginning of the wakes songs: a pilgrim with a harp walks in the centre of the decorative band. Wakes and pilgrims are frequent and rewarding themes of sacred songs in the Baroque period

228

Piſné a Letanye w Křjžowé Dni na Proceſy
Za wſſeliké wedle Czaſu potřeby a důležitoſti/ Pautnjkům na Swaté Mjſta Ceſtau gdaucým k pobožnému rozgjmánj a ſpjwánj.

Gako: Ačkoliwěk lidſká chwála/ ꝛč.

Geden začjná. Wſſycknj. Geden.

Radůg ſe Panno čiſtá/ Zdráwas Marya/ pleſey Rodičko Božſká/ Alleluja/ pozdrawenás Marya/ pros za nás ſwého Syna.

Panno Koruno Panen. Zdráwas Marya. Y Láſky Božj pramen/ Alleluja/ pozdrawenás Marya/ pros za nás ſwého Syna.

¶ Matko wſſechněch wěřjcých. Zdráwas Marya. Wſſech Boha milugjcých/ Alleluja/ prozdrawenás/ ꝛč. ¶ Matko ſwaté naděge. Zdráwas Marya. A způſobce pokoge/ Alleluja/ prozdrawenás/ ꝛč. ¶ Tys Rág prawé rozkoſſe. Zdráwas Marya. A Žiwot naſſý Duſſe/ Alleluja/ pozd:/ ꝛč. Autočiſſtě gſy Měſto. Zdráwas Marya. Jeruzaléma ſláwo/ Alleluja/ pozdra:/ ꝛč. ¶ Pána Kryſta Swatyně. Zdráwas Marya. Ržebřjk přjmý do Nebe/ Alleluja/ pozdra: ꝛč. ¶ Tys čiſtoty Zrcadlo. Zdráwas Marya. Keř Mogžjſſe diwadlo/ Alleluja/ pozdra: ꝛč. ¶ O Lilium přewonné!

Kk 2

Zdrá-

The Baroque church of St. Thomas is located at the corner of the present-day Letenská Street and the Lesser Quarter (Malostranské) square. The church with monastery for the Augustine hermit order was established as soon as in the 13th century and has been reconstructed many times since then. Today it can boast especially of the monumental frescoes by Wenceslas Lawrence Reiner on the vault and the valuable organ from 1730 produced by master John Francis Fassmann

HAEC

The Lobkowicz palace in Vlašská Street in the Lesser Quarter dates back to the 18th century. It is the work of the famous High-Baroque architect Giovanni Battista Alliprandi. Also this showy noble palace had its productions of the aristocratic orchestra in the Baroque time, particularly in the pretentious festivals and balls

eventually a rather special tactics: they planted new texts with pro-Catholic contents on the popular tunes of the original Reformation songs. A big official hymnbook with tunes for one voice was compiled by the Jesuit Matthew Wenceslas Šteyer (1630–1692); its six editions from 1683 to 1764 in Prague document the intensity of this anti-Reformation endeavour. On the other hand, the hymnbook Capella regia musicalis (The Song and Music Royal Chapel) by Wenceslas Holan Rovenský (1644–1718) published in Prague in 1693 represents songs created in the typical Baroque homophony.

The development and social application of the main Baroque musical forms – opera, oratorio and concertant instrumental music – were unequal in Prague and legged behind the development of these genres elsewhere in Europe. At least a slight bloom was reached in Prague by instrumental music. It was characterized by concertant alternating of musical sections played solo and by a group of instruments. One of the compositions using as one of the first the new style is Magnificat by John Sixt of Lerchefels (died 1629) who already in his young days came in touch with the latest streams of the new music in the Prague orchestra of Rudolph II and later was active also as a high religious official. In the environment of the Rudolph's orchestra he got acquainted with the works of the Italian masters and adapted his musical expression to the new concept.

The church of Our Lady Below Chain in Lázeňská Street in the Lesser Quarter belonged in the Baroque period to places renowned for musical productions. Even today this temple decorated with pictures of the excellent painter Charles Škréta is a place of frequent performances of significant musical ensembles – here it is a production of the group "Asperula odorata" within the framework of the advent concerts

Even under the unfavourable circumstances of the re-Catholicizing political situation and in its modest conditions Prague tried to keep pace with the development of music elsewhere in the world. Significant domestic composers Adam Michna of Otradovice (about

This cathedral cupola belongs to the church of St. Francis Seraphimus in the building of the General Office of Knights of the Cross at Křížovnické square. Musical productions in this church ranked among the best known and most frequently visited also due to their so-called sepolcrum which was Easter oratorio played in the Lent period and which was accessible to all strata of the population

1600–1676) or Paul Joseph Vejvanovský (1640–1693) who were close to the application of the new style means did not work directly in Prague but they influenced the musical life of Prague by their compositions (the former was an organ player in Jidřichův Hradec, the latter was the head of the orchestra of the Olomouc bishop Charles Liechtenstein-Castelcorn at Kroměříž). Michna's Česká mariánská muzika (The Czech Music for Our Lady, published in Prague in 1647), Loutna česká (The Czech Lute, Prague 1653), Officium vespertinum (Prague 1648), Sacra et litaniae (Prague 1654) and Svatoroční muzika (Holy Year Music, Prague 1661) are valuable documents of continuing Czech musical creativity in the Baroque period. From among the works by Vejvanovský, particularly his brilliant sonatas for clarino (trompette) instruments, cathedral sonatas and suites for various instrument ensembles had success in Prague.

A popular form of the Baroque music was the so-called school theatre produced in Prague in the Jesuit and Piarist colleges and in monasteries of other orders. The function of this theatre was anti-Reformatory religious and pedagogical and music played generally a significant role in it. Most of the plays were performed by the students in Latin, exceptionally in Czech or German, and took place mainly on the occasion of celebrations of religious holidays or in honour of religious officials. In the large Prague colleges they were usually participated by as much as a hundred persons, their scene decorations were showy so as to have effect both on the noble and common audience. By means of this theatre the inhabitants of Prague got familiar with the fate of Christ and with the lives of the martyrs and saints. A foremost place in this repertoire was occupied, in particular, by plays about St. Wenceslas and St. John of Nepomuk. Music for these plays, or melodrama as they were called at that time, was fulfilling a demanding artistic mission. Among the composers of such music we can find also the former Jesuit college student and later musician of the Saxon court John Dismas Zelenka (1679–1745). On the occasion of coronation as the Czech king, the performance of Zelenka's allegorical play called Sub olea pacis et palma virtutis (Under the Twig of Peace and Palm of Virtue) in the Clementinum in 1723 was attended even by the Emperor Charles VI ruling at the Hapsburg throne in 1711–1740. Such an event, however, was an exception in the Baroque Prague rather than a rule.

Beside monasteries, the main centres of cathedral music in the 17th and 18th centuries were churches. There were many of them throughout Prague. Their musicians often competed with each other by means of their repertoires existing only in manuscripts. The most dignified and most important position among them was occupied by St. Vitus's Cathedral, particularly under its choir-leader Nicholas Francis Xaver Wencela (about 1643–1722), the author of a big collection of cathedral works (e. g. Flores verni, Prague 1699). The key specialization were compositions of vocal-instrumental type alternating homophony with polyphony, solos with choirs accompanied with various musical instruments. Wencela already used major-minor tonality instead of the old church modes. In the Prague church of the monastery of Knights of the Cross we can meet double-

The bronze statue of the Baroque saint from 1683 is the oldest one at Charles Bridge. The silver Baroque tombstone of John of Nepomuk in St. Vitus's cathedral upon the project of the architect Fischer of Erlach dates back to 1733–1736

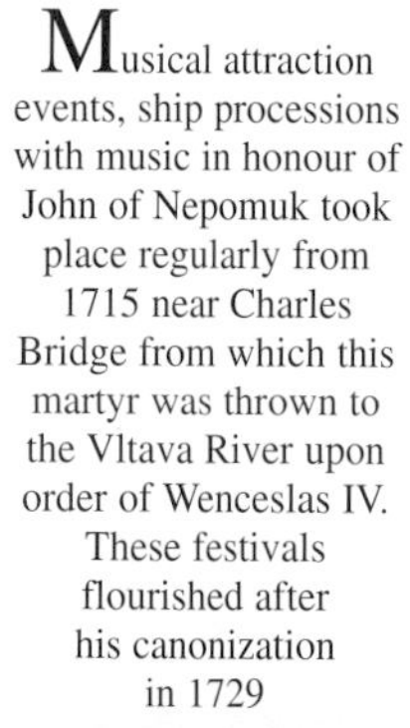

Musical attraction events, ship processions with music in honour of John of Nepomuk took place regularly from 1715 near Charles Bridge from which this martyr was thrown to the Vltava River upon order of Wenceslas IV. These festivals flourished after his canonization in 1729

choir vocal technique for the sake of which two opposite choirs were built in the church. Choral singing of this type was popular in Europe and showed also influence on the foremost vocal art of Prague.

As already suggested, cathedral music was played mostly by a small number of musicians. According to historical reports, about 1727 the famous stable ensemble in the Prague Loretta had only 13 musicians consisting of a choir-leader, an organist, 3 violinists, a violist, an oboe player and 6 vocalists. Buglers, timpani players and a double-bass player were presumably invited from case to case from among voluntary amateurish musicians which was common almost in all ensembles of that time. The St. Vitus's musicians were no exception: in 1710 the musical ensemble had 8 vocalists and 6 instrumentalists, in 1716 in the Strahov church only 2 young descant singers, 4 adult singers, an organ player and 2 buglers were paid. Together with invited guest musicians including singers, the number of members of the Baroque ensembles usually did not exceed 16 to 20 performers. This composition of ensembles was usual in a great number of churches and monasteries in Prague which competed mainly with each other in which one is able to perform better the demanding figural music. The best known and most-frequented were the musical productions of the church of Francis Seraphimus in the monastery of Knights of the Cross near Charles Bridge, in the Jesuit church of St. Saviour in the Clementinum, in St. Nicholas's church in the Lesser Quarter, in St. Ignaz's church in the New Town, in St. James's church in Minorite monastery, in the church of Our Lady Below the Chain in Hospitaler monastery, in St. Michael's church in Servites monastery, in St. Nicholas's church in Benedictine monastery, in the church of Our Lady Before Týn, in St. Martin's church, in

St. Gallus's church in the Old Town belongs to the oldest temples of Prague. It was adapted in the Baroque style in the early 18th century by the architects Giovanni Orsi, John Santini-Aichl and Paul Ignaz Bayer. Of great interest is the front wall in the style of the Illusive Baroque. Like in other Prague churches, also here music and sacred singing could be heard in the aisle for centuries

the church of Our Lady at Strahov, in St. Vitus's cathedral and, naturally, in the already mentioned Loretta whose chimes of Virgin Mary by Peter Naumann of 1694 became a famous attraction.

Despite all this the Baroque period had a passion for showy festivals in which music played an important role. However, if a choir or orchestra had a great number of members it was always something extraordinary and the witnesses or historians did not fail to record this in their reports. When in 1715 in the Lesser Quarter the Trinity column was consecrated litanies and Te Deum were performed on that occasion by 200 musicians. On the occasion of sanctification of John of Nepomuk in 1729 the production in front of the Saint's statue near St. Henry's church was performed by 40 musicians and Caldar's mass was performed in St. Vitus's cathedral by 300 musicians divided into two choirs. The festive procession carried out the same day was accompanied by a total of 56 buglers. The canonization festivities in behalf of the new country patron took ten days and were celebrated not only in Prague but throughout the country. Even earlier, from 1715, i. e. fourteen years before his sanctification, musical attraction events, ship processions with music in honour of John of Nepomuk took place regularly near Charles Bridge from which there was a wonderful view of Prague and the calmly running Vltava. The festivals were performed mainly in the places where John of Nepomuk was allegedly thrown to the Vltava. They usually started with flourishes performed by several groups of buglers and timpani players and then litanies, smaller cantatas and Regina coeli were produced in festively decorated ships. The compositions written for these purposes were called musica navalis – i. e. naval music. Particularly brass instruments were used abundantly in this type of music. Here, an inventive approach can be seen in the works by the Prague composers John Zach (1699–1773), Wenceslas G. Jacob (1685–1734) and Simon Brixi (1693–1735).

The tradition of this "musica navalis" was preserved in Prague for many decades up to 1786 when even the famous St. John ship processions were cancelled. It was considered as Prague speciality that there was a "procession" of decorated ships going from the district of Podskalí to the centre of the city with musicians mostly with brass instruments playing music suitable for these cultural attractions. Great many of inhabitants of Prague were listening to them from the Vltava embankment. Unfortunately, their repertoire has not been preserved but for only a few isolated cases.

It was not until the early 18th century that opera works of the so-called Naples school started to gain ground in Prague to a greater degree. They are represented by the names of Leonardo Vinci (1690–1727), Johann Adolf Hasse (1699–1783), Giovanni Battista Pergolesi (1710–1736) and others. The Czech composers under the influence of these authors not only assimilated and adopted the principles of the high Baroque music but, moreover, enriched their works by the original Czech melodiousness while applying a simpler concept approach in oratorios and cantatas since they had to count on the more modest possibilities of the Prague cathedral and monastery instrumental ensembles.

An evening concert in the open air at the most beautiful and smallest square of Prague – Křížovnické square – in front of the church of St. Francis Seraphimus in which grandiose musical and song productions took place just like in other significant churches. One of the most precious collections of musical works in Prague was gathered in the church in the past, especially from the 17th and 18th centuries

The year 1627 was significant by the fact that during the coronation of Ferdinand III (1608–1657) as Czech king, a pastoral opera was performed in Prague with music by the Italian composer Giovanni Battista Buonamente (died 1642). In 1680 the Prague Castle court theatre produced several operas – among them a witty comedy by the Italian composer Antonio Draghi (1635–1700) La Patienza di Socrate con due mogli (Socrates' Patience with Two Wives) which was for the first time that a comic opera was performed in Prague.

The crucial turning point in the development of the musical life, however, can be considered only the year 1723 when during the coronation of Charles VI as Czech king the Vienna court theatre performed in Prague the opera Constanza e Fortezza (Constancy and Force) by the court composer Johann Joseph Fux (1660–1741). According to the contemporary reports, this performance

One of the most beautiful areas of the Clementinum complex is the "oratory greater than the Latin congregation" now called Mirror Chapel (or Mirror Hall) the building of which was finished in 1724. The project designer was Francis Maxmilian Kaňka. The interior is decorated with stucco with mirror inlays and of great interest also is the sculptural decoration, ceiling paintings and pictures. Today the chapel is used also as a concert hall – in this case it is the performance of the famous Stamic quartet

At the turn of the 17th and 18th centuries the development of the Prague High Baroque was contributed by Marco Antonio Canevalle: he built the church for the New Town nunnery of the Ursula order. The side front of the church is today applied as the main facade facing Národní Street. The visitors are strongly impressed by the wonderful interior of the church. Music and sacred singing can be heard in the church even today – here the Prague ČVUT Choir and Hanover Choir and the chamber "Orchestra Puellarum Pragensis"

The church of St. James, an originally Gothic building reconstructed in the Baroque period was provided with organ from the workshop of Abraham Storck of Loket in 1702. That period was also the time of the blossom of the musical life connected, in particular, with the activity of the composer and organ player Bohuslav Matthew Černohorský who was appreciated by his contemporaries as well as the musicians of today. The church located at the corner of the streets Jakubská and Malá Štupartská is renowned for its organ concerts even today. Here we can see a performance of the choir of St. James and the orchestra Cantores Pragenses

(played twice on 28 August and 2 September) produced a massive impression. Musical historians even rank it among the peak events in the history of European opera as such. The festivity and significance of the performance was magnified by the fact that it was this coronation that the Czech people bent their political hopes to because it was a promise of a radical change of social life in the Czech lands. There were about three hundred of performers on the stage from which a hundred Italian singers with excellent voices and about two hundred instrumentalists selected from the whole Europe. The auditorium was built for four thousand people and the so-called illusory scene considered as one of the peaks of the Baroque scene design was provided by the court architect H. Galli-Bibiena. It was located on the training field of the so-called Summer Riding School near Prague Castle. Instead of the composer Fux who fell ill this exceptional performan-

ce was conducted two times by the Vienna court orchestra member Antonio Caldara (about 1670–1736). On this occasion, a virtual elite of musicians from the whole Central Europe came to Prague, including A. Caldara, J. D. Zelenka, J. J. Quantz, G. Tartini, F. M. Veracini, F. Benda, G. Muffat, S. Weiss, F. Conti and others.

Although the Czech nobility spent most of the year in Vienna in order not to lose contact with the ruler's court they built splendid palaces in Prague which – be it for a short time in the year only – they filled with rich social and cultural life. This concentration of nobility palaces in Prague was exceptional and there is no place else in Europe that we could meet something like that. Most of these edifices were artistically imposing and economically demanding not only during their construction but also in their daily operation. Therefore, with the increased interest in the representation of the Prague

nobility it was logical that in this time there was a gradual growth in the interest in opera.

Opera Constanza e Fortezza was not the only one work played during the coronation festivities. Also the operas by Caldara and Conti were performed but these did not have such success as the work by Fux. Under the influence of these grandiose festivals the famous patron of arts Count Francis Anthony Sporck (1662–1738) hired in 1724 the company of the Italian impresario Antonio Denzi (?) which during ten years performed about 60 operas of both renowned and less known Italian composers. This company had 8 singers and 11 instrumentalists. The activity of the company started on 22 October, 1724 by the opera Orlando furioso (Furious Orlando) by the orchestra conductor G. A. Bioni (1698–1739). Baron Sichingen elaborated for this stage also an opera dealing with a Czech theme Praga nascente da Libussa e Primislav (Prague founded by Libuše and Přemysl) presented in 1734. Nevertheless, the artistic peak in the repertoire of Denzi's company were the operas by Vivaldi (1678–1741) who hired singers in Italy for Denzi's company and provided it with new opera works for Prague. After Denzi's leaving Prague in 1738 the role of theatre impresario was taken over by Santo Lapis. In 1743–1746 another Italian company was active here. This Mingotti's company was focused, in particular, on a repertoire of Naples composers and by their interpretation qualities it ranked among the best companies in Europe.

Beside opera under the Italian impresarios in Prague there was a bloom of the so-called sepolcrum which was Easter oratorium played in the Lent period when theatre was forbidden. It was performed in monasteries and churches in the Clementinum, in St. Nicholas's church in the Old Town and in St. Nicholas's church in the Lesser Quarter, in Emaus monastery, in St. Giles's church, in Strahov monastery and in the monastery of Knights of the Cross. The advantage of these productions was that access was allowed to all social strata of the population.

The Italian sculptor Ottavio Mosto came to Prague by the end of the 17th century. His Prague works include three stucco reliefs in the facade of the cathedral of St. James in the Old Town depicting scenes from the lives of St. James, St. Francis of Assisi and St. Anthony of Padua.

The first two works include cherubs with musical instruments. Here are details from the reliefs

A significant community in the 17th and 18th centuries in Prague was formed by the Jews. Their number achieved one-fourth of the total number of inhabitants which certainly was reflected in the musical culture of the city. Generally they produced purpose-oriented music. Groups comprising two violinists, a double-bass player and a cymbalom player performed music at betrothals, weddings, christening parties and funerals. They were cheap and were good in playing for dance. The Christian musicians, however, did not want to reconcile themselves with such competitors, which sometimes was a source of anti-Semitic tension. Therefore, it was even necessary that Cardinal Ernest Albrecht Harrach (1598–1667) as well as the Emperor Leopold I ruling in 1657–1705 had to intervene in favour of the Jews in order to confirm the old right of the Jewish musicians to play for all the Christians. Beside dance music the Prague Jews produced in their synagogues also music for divine services and artistic instrumental music. In 1716 they organized a festive concert in honour of the birth of the imperial prince participated by 9 buglers, 8 violinists, 4 horn players, 4 timpani players and an organist.

While the Baroque in Europe has its musical representatives in the personalities of A. Vivaldi, J. S. Bach and F. G. Händel, the Czech lands also have their authors who under more favourable conditions surely would play a significant role in the development of the Czech music. There were many talents but they were lacking conditions for making their mark in Prague. We can mention here at least the two most significant composers who were actual creative personalities. The first one was Bohuslav Matthew Černohorský (1684–1742), member of the Prague Minorite order who had to live mostly abroad, mainly in Italy where after twenty years of active work he was called Il Padre Boemo (Father Czech). Černohorský worked in Prague only occasionally, mainly as organist in St. James's church in the Old Town where he often was in touch with Simon Brixi. It was a tragedy, however, for the composer and the Czech music that most of the works of Bohuslav Matthew Černohorský (with the exception of several organ fugues and choral works) had burnt in the fire of St. James's church. The torso of his work suggests that he was an author of extraordinary artistic format.

The other important author of the Czech Baroque music was the already mentioned John Dismas Zelenka who studied music in the Jesuits college in Prague but later spent most of his life abroad. Although he tried to maintain the closest possible contacts with Prague and his work was played here from time to time this artist devoted most of his potency to double-bass playing in the court orchestra of the Saxon king in Dresden. It could be considered a historical injustice that he was not granted the honour to become the court composer despite the fact that he was an author whose exceptional art was respected even by Johann Sebastian Bach. Even after 250 years from his death John Dismas Zelenka ranks among the most distinctive personalities of the Czech musical Baroque.

The monumental cathedral of St. James in the Old Town of Prague whose two unequally tall spires are towering over the surrounding roofs is famous for organ productions and concerts of cathedral music. The tall and long aisle promotes organ sound. This is one of the reasons why the regular musical programmes are frequently visited

In the period of Classicism

In contrast to the musical Baroque where there were considerable differences between musical work for the upper classes of society and the love for singing of the people, this disproportion is being levelled in the period of the musical Classicism. The influence of folk music on artificial work was so strong in the new era that the music of all social strata suddenly acquired new and yet to a certain degree common style features. The reasons why the development went in this direction were multiple. In the period from about 1740 to 1810 new forms of musical life began to come gradually to the fore. In Prague, however, this process was delayed and started not until about the end of the 18th century. On the one hand, the focal point of musical productions shifted

The House of Blue Ship (No. 464 U Modré lodi) in Melantrichova Street is now in its appearance of 1740 when it was the home of Joseph Mysliveček who was an older friend of Wolfgang Amadeus Mozart. He belonged to the most important predecessors of Mozart in the period of Classicism. His music won fans in his homeland and, particularly, in Italy where he was called "Il Boemo" and "Venatori" or "Il divino Boemo". The significant Czech composer Joseph Mysliveček lived in 1737–1781

The Baroque facade of the monastery and hospital of the Brethren of Mercy. The monastery with the hospital was known, besides its primary mission, also by musical activities and was connected with a number of musicians, such as the disciples of Joseph Haydn. Francis Xaver Brixi died in this hospital on 14 October, 1771. Musical history reminds us also of the name of John Theobald Held (1770–1851), physician, the hospital chief physician and excellent musician and composer

from the cathedral environment and closed monastery rooms to opera theatres and concert halls which were more accessible to the city and small-town social strata. On the other hand, musicians got rid of their footman obligations in the nobility orchestras and became free people and professionals. At the same time, the Classicism in music instigated the occurrence of many new musical forms derived from the cyclic sonata form, i. e. music of the type of four-move symphonies, solo concertos, various forms of chamber music including string quartet and woodwind quintet. However, opera and other big forms of music, too subordinated themselves to the new, classically proportionate style. Homophonic and cantabile nature of music, symmetry of melody structure, contrast themes and their new manner of development give hitherto unknown features to the musical expression whose top representatives at the end of this development period were real masters, such as Joseph Haydn (1732–1809), Wolfgang Amadeus Mozart (1756–1791) and Ludwig van Beethoven (1770–1827).

The halls of the Clam-Gallas palace were full of music especially in the period when the significant patron of arts Count Christian Clam-Gallas married Comtesse Josephine Clary who was an excellent mandolin player. This performance in the wonderful hall shows the Prague Telemann Quartet

During the second half of the 18th century under the influence of the economic weakening of the Czech nobility, its orchestras performing instrumental music were dissolved, e. g. the Czernin, Kinský, archbishopric orchestras, etc. This tradition gradually finishes its days even in the famous orchestras with rich repertoire, such as those of Count Clam-Gallas and Count Johann Joseph Pachta.

With the new social situation and with the new forms of life of the aristocratic circles, Italian musical companies performing opera took roots in Prague from 1724 at the end of the Baroque era up to 1807. However, the life in these "serious" operas (so-called opera seria) coming to this country mainly from Italy had almost nothing to do with real life. This new art served chiefly to the celebration of the ruler families and amusement of the nobility, dealing with mythological themes, using castrates for perfect singing performances in mere technical and virtuoso terms. Theatre was not only a place for the production of musical art as we know it today but also a place of social life. Its characteristic feature was the institute of the opera impresario who organized opera productions and made his best to accommodate the tastes and needs of aristocracy who subsidized the theatre houses, hired theatre boxes where the nobility members entertained themselves and received visits and only from time to time listened to the artists singing in their honour.

After the dissolution of Denzi's company and the shortly working Sporck's opera as mentioned above, the theatre "V Kotcích" (sometimes called Nationaltheater) was established in Prague in 1737. It was a significant theatre because it made a substantial mark in the musical life of Prague. Its first impresario was Santo Lapis, Italian composer and experienced theatre entrepreneur. Unfortunately, we have only few reports on its re-

The streets of the Old Town were lined with imposing Baroque buildings of the foremost aristocrats. The most monumental of them, the Clam–Gallas palace was built in 1719–1723 upon order of John Wenceslas Gallas, the viceroy of Naples, on the basis of the project of the Viennese architect Fischer of Erlach. The fronts are decorated by huge portals with balconies supported by pairs of Herculeses produced by Matthias Bernard Braun. The Clam-Gallas palace had a theatre hall and its active orchestra put a polish on the social standard of the owner

pertoire but we know that intermezzo of the famous opera La serva padrona (Maidservant of the Lady) by Giovanni Battisto Pergolesi (1710–1736) was played in Prague in 1744 which, as a matter of fact, was the first staged musical work in the genre of comic opera buffa. As compared to serious opera (seria) the popularity of opera buffa increased also in Prague because thanks to it characters from the people's environment appeared on the stage – now there were not only gods from myths and legends but also common people, such as valets and maidservants of the counts and countesses with their sharp tongue and wit, characters of the burgher class with their daily problems and comic plots. Accordingly, also in singing the comic opera started to prefer natural voices and natural singing to artificial and technical pompousness of the singer stars many of whom were castrates.

It was a merit of the musical and theatrical life of Prague that since the half of the 18th century also this city – even though not being the residence of the ruler's court – indulged itself in all the significant works of contemporary Italy which, in this field, was regarded as the cradle and model of contemporary opera theatre. An important role in this was played, in particular, by the Italian impresarios G. B. Locatelli, A. Mingotti, G. Molinari, G. Bustelli, P. Bondini, D. Guardasoni and others. As the conductor of Locatelli company in V Kotcích theatre (1749–50 and 1751–52) Christoph Willibald

The Bretfeld palace is located at the corner of the streets Jánský vršek and Nerudova. It was built in 1765 by the architect John George Wirch for Joseph, the free lord of Bretfeld. The owner was a famous host who organized costly balls. In 1787 his guests included Wolfgang Amadeus Mozart

The Thun-Leslie palace in the Lesser Quarter which is the residence of the British Embassy today was reconstructed according to the plans of the architect Giovanni Battista Alliprandi in 1716–1727. The courtyard wing in the Romantic Gothic style dates back to the middle of the 19th century. The palace is known by the fact that Wolfgang Amadeus Mozart lived here with his wife Constance during his first visit to Prague in January 1787

180
14

The Estates Theatre (former Nosticz theatre), the first stable theatre building in Prague was built according to the plans of the architect Anthony Haffenecker in the area behind St. Gallus's church in the Old Town. Anthony Haffenecker is the most important creative personality of the beginnings of the Prague Classicism. The influence of the French Classicist school can be seen in his works. The Estates Theatre is connected inseparably with Wolfgang Amadeus Mozart and his operas The Marriage of Figaro and Don Giovanni

Gluck (1714–1787) performed his pre-reform operas Ezio (1750) and Issipile (1752). German comic opera called Singspiel became a significant rival to the opera of the Italian companies and to the Italian style. This was especially true under the directorship of Karl Wahr in V Kotcích theatre.

In Prague there were smaller theatres devoted to the Italian repertoire, too. For instance, Count Thun provided the Italian company of Pasquale Bondini with the so-called Small Theatre in his Lesser Quarter palace in 1781–1784. In 1786 Vlastenské (Patriotic) theatre was established in Prague which was a professional theatre with bilingual performances but it had not live long.

Mozart finished the opera Don Giovanni in Prague. He prepared it himself in the Estates Theatre and conducted its first night on 29 October, 1787. This work of his received great response. Prague was granted an exceptional opera work which is unconventional not only by its music but also by its remarkable topic. The scene staged in the Estates Theatre is from the present performance of the opera

In parallel with these more or less modest theatres, in 1783 in the square in front of the Carolinum a new, representative, then modern theatre was built at the costs of Count Frederic Nosticz and later supported by the Czech estates (hence the name Stavovské, i. e. Theatre of the Estates). Its architects were Anthony Hafenecker and Count Künigl. It was hired by Bondini for his company and as one of few Italian impresarios also here he managed to maintain a good artistic standard of his musical productions. It was a custom in Nosticz theatre that opera was played three times a week and drama was played the other days.

In the opera ensembles of the Italian musical companies which always settled in Prague for a time there were not only foreigners. The impresario and his singer stars came chiefly from Italy and other neighbouring countries but most of the musicians were local people, practical musicians

Today, Bertramka serves as a memorial of the Dušeks and Wolfgang Amadeus Mozart. A part of the interior from Mozart's time and the corresponding equipment produce the atmosphere of the stay of the great composer. Prague enjoyed Mozart's presence and his musical success as an artistic exceptionality

The interior of the Bertramka villa. The performance of contemporary artists in period costumes is an attractive memory of the Prague world premiere of the opera Don Giovanni and its author who was given an exceptionally warm acceptance by the musical Prague. Here we can see the production of the Original Musical Theatre Prague of famous operatic arias

who were hired for the operation of the theatre. The intensity of the Italian speaking theatre companies culminated in the 1780s and then at the turn of the century they were replaced by the burgher and folk Singspiel, vaudeville and play with songs which are works performed mostly in German or Czech.

The peak activities of the Italian companies in Prague are connected also with the visits of Wolfgang Amadeus Mozart in the Czech capital. They contributed not only to a greater fame of the young composer in the Czech lands but gave, at the same time, the best certificate to the musical taste of the Prague audience since it recognized the genius in Mozart that must be honoured. The first success of Mozart's work in Prague is connected with the Singspiel play Die Entführung aus dem Serail (Abduction from the Palace) which was probably performed in 1782 by the company of K. Wahr in V Kotcích theatre and next season it was played in the newly opened Nosticz theatre. These, however, were only the first gleams of the composer's popularity the climax of which came later. Thanks to P. Bondini Prague saw in 1786 one of Mozart's hitherto best operas The Marriage of Figaro which at that time was not accepted by the Vienna audience. It was performed in Nosticz theatre and brought the author a grandiose success. Tradition says that its melodies were sung by the people just for fun, that they were played by harp players and folk musicians in the streets and in pubs. For the great but still very

Bertramka, which became world known for the stay of Wolfgang Amadeus Mozart, is the old manor in the district of Smíchov from the end of the 17th century called after is former owner. It was extended during a Classicist reconstruction in the second half of the 18th century. From 1774 the house was possessed by Mozart's Prague friends Mr. and Mrs. Dušeks. In the garden of Bertramka we can see the bust of Wolfgang Amadeus Mozart by the sculptor Thomas Seidan from 1876

The wonderful Baroque cathedral of St. Nicholas in the Lesser Quarter was in 1791 the place of the biggest Mozart ceremony in Europe – the funeral event in the memory of the death of the artist. The production was organized by the Prague theatre orchestra as an evidence of respect and admiration of Mozart. Requiem in Es major by F.A. Rössler (Rosetti) was performed by 120 musicians headed by the popular singer Josephine Dušková and conducted by John Joseph Strobach

young composer this success was a unanimous satisfaction for the wrongs and non-acceptance in Vienna. After the success of The Marriage of Figaro, the resourceful and enterprising Bondini ordered at once a new opera by Mozart – Don Giovanni upon the libretto by Lorenzo da Ponte. During the year the composer did not accomplish the work completely – he finished it only in Prague after his arrival on 4 October and he was said to finish the overture only during the rehearsals for its world premiere. He prepared and conducted it himself in the Prague theatre on 29 October, 1787. This success overcame all expectations. So far, none of Mozart's works – with the exception of The Marriage of Figaro last year – had reaped such a huge success. There was a presentiment in everyone, be it skilled musician or simple viewer that here, Prague got an entirely exceptional opera work which was a real gem, a musical drama with living people, a work which was unconventional not only in terms of its music but by its remarkable topic as well. Literally, Don Giovanni has became the opera of all operas despite the fact that for a long time it was only Prague that understood its greatness and artistic exceptionality.

During his visits to Prague W. A. Mozart often stayed in the friendly family of the composer Francis Xaver Dušek for whose wife, the famous singer Josephine Dušková (1754–1824) he wrote several remarkable arias the best known of which is "Bella mia fiamma". The Prague residence of the Dušeks, their Bertramka villa became the memorial of Mozart's stays and success in Prague. Rumour has it that in the time of Mozart's stay in Prague in 1787 Count Johann Joseph Pachta ordered some new dance compositions. Mozart promised to do the work but postponed it permanently so that finally Pachta thought out a trick: he invited the composer to his palace (most probably in Mikulandská Street) to a salon where there was no society only a piano with ink and note paper. According to the message of the Count, Mozart was not to be released from this "jail" until he wrote the promised work. And so the author composed Six German Dances – with the title "Sechs Teutsche".

In 1791 not long before the composer's death, Prague, namely its estates ordered another work by Mozart on the occasion of the coronation of the Austrian Emperor Leopold II as Czech king (he ruled shortly 1790–1792) – the opera La clemenza di Tito (The Benignity of Titus) upon libretto by E. Mazzola according to Metastasius. Its premiere took place on 6 September, 1891 in Nosticz theatre but it found favourable acceptance neither in the imperial court nor in wider population. The Queen and Empress ascribed the new work as "Porcheira tedesca" – a German mess! When disappointed

Mozart returned to Vienna he wrote his clarinet concerto and sent it for the premiere to Prague but he did not live to see its performance. He died too soon. Prague honoured the memory of Mozart on 14 December, 1791 by a huge mourning celebration in the Lesser Quarter church of St. Nicholas. It was one of the greatest commemoration ceremonies organized as testimony of unlimited respect of the Prague inhabitants to Mozart. Such a great ceremony in memory of the composer had not taken place in any other European metropolis. The musical programme was conducted by John Joseph Strobach (1731–1794), the St. Nicholas's church choir-leader and director of theatre orchestra who for the interpretation of Requiem by Francis Anthony Rössler (1746–1792) known abroad by the name Rosetti, hired 120 musicians headed by the popular singer Josephine Dušková admired also by Mozart. "A catafalque stood in the centre of the church, three groups of trumpets and drums rang in a dampened sound..., thousands of tears dropped down for Mozart who through his celestial harmonies tuned our hearts to the finest feelings so many times..." – these were the words by which the contemporary press described the commemoration ceremony.

Prague saw another tremendous success after the author's death in connection with Mozart's last Singspiel The Magic Flute in 1794. This work, in particular, was designed for the common layers of audience which accepted it at once. There are few operas that got such an attention in one city. In Prague, it was interpreted almost simultaneously in several languages – in the German original as well as in the Italian and Czech translations. It was remarkable too that the Czech translation was made by the then most significant Czech theatre worker Wenceslas Thám (1765–1816). In this form the work was played in the Patriotic theatre in the former Hybernian monastery. Yet another fact is connected with Mozart's name: the performance of his last opera La clemenza di Tito in April 1807 ended definitely the era of the Italian opera in Prague lasting 83 years. In the future, the Prague audience preferred German Singspiel and Czech plays with songs which was a fact that the Italian companies were not able to cope with.

Prague has achieved another pre-eminence in connection with Mozart: here, the first monograph on the composer was written by the writer dealing with music history and a member of a Czech schoolmaster family from the town of Sadská, Francis X. Němeček (1766–1849). This small but authentic work (called Lebensbeschreibung des K. K. Kapellmeisters W. A. Mozart, 1st version 1798, 2nd version 1808) is based chiefly on the personal experiences of the author and memories of the contemporaries. Up to our days it belongs among the most substantial early works about W. A. Mozart.

We can say without exaggeration that Mozart's opera and the composer's cult in Prague instigated the desire of the Czech composers to try to create a specifically Czech opera. Unfortunately, none of them – e. g. F. V. Tuček (1755–1820), A. F. Vojtíšek (1771– about 1820), A. Volánek (1761–1817) and others – had so much vigour to make this generous target successfully come true. In 1804 the Czech opera even had to leave Nosticz theatre, now called the Estates Theatre because the presence of the common Czech people in the theatre rooms did not accommodate the noble aristocratic society.

Prague had the honour to be visited twice by Ludwig van Beethoven but the author was not here to conduct a premiere of some of his works

The grave of the Dušeks at the Lesser Quarter cemetery near their Bertramka house the guest of which was also W.A. Mozart. Francis Xaver Dušek (1731–1799) was a composer and Josephine Dušková (1754–1824) was a recognized singer for whom Mozart wrote two remarkable arias

but as interpreter of his piano pieces. His productions in 1796–1798 were limited to the environment of aristocratic salons where Beethoven had a lot of friends. During his first stay he composed a scene and aria "Ah perfido" as well as Sonatina and Theme with variations for mandolin and harpsichord for the excellent mandolin player Comtesse Josephine Clary, later married with the significant patron of arts Count Christian Clam-Gallas. Like in the case of the first monograph about Mozart produced in Prague, Prague was the first city to contribute to the evaluation of Beethoven's personality. As soon as in 1829, i. e. only two years after the composer's death, a book written in the German language by J. A. Schlosser was published here in which the author confesses frankly his admiration of the composer's works.

The Lesser Town cemetery where the significant Czech musician Wenceslas John Tomášek was buried in 1850. Tomášek is said to be a sort of a connecting link between the Czech Classicism and the work of Bedřich Smetana belonging already to the nationalist-marked style period

From the 1720s great oratorio works started to be performed regularly in Prague. In this field, the main centre was the order of Knights of the Cross which had at its disposal the wonderful Baroque cathedral near Charles Bridge. Here, the performances took place of oratorio works with Latin and German texts by the authors Antonio Caldara (about 1670–1736), Niccolo Porpora (1686–1768), Johann A. Hasse (1699–1783) and others and from among the domestic authors by the composers Francis Xaver Brixi, Joseph Sehling (1710–1756), Francis W. Habermann (1706–1783), John Dismas Zelenka, Joseph A. Štěpán (1726–1797), Joseph Mysliveček (1737–1781) and many others. This tradition, however, did not survive the century. It was stopped by the reforms of the Empress Maria Theresa and her son Joseph II which, on the one hand, contributed to the economic revival of the Czech lands but, on the other hand, disrupted heavily the hitherto favourably developing musical life and musical school system. To restrict the luxury and splendour of the religious rites including religious processions it was prohibited already in 1754 to use trumpets and drums and twelve years later even the musician guilds and brotherhoods of men of letters were forbidden. For musicians of various kinds this meant that they had to look for new jobs which often was the reason why they left the country. The abolishment of the Jesuit order in 1773 inflicted a bad blow also to the musical school system not only in Prague but in all Czech lands, in towns and in the country since Jesuits (beside Premonstratensians) gave great importance to music lessons in their order and the schools controlled by them.

The restriction of cathedral music where due to the reforms the instrumental accompaniment within the framework of the divine service rites was admissible only on festive occasions (otherwise, the accompaniment was strictly limited to organ only) produced a pressure on new forms of musical life – on the establishment and functioning of public concerts and the municipal opera. In Prague these initial efforts to perform concert productions were very modest. Many years had to pass before the development came to independent concert halls built only for that very purpose. The meaning of the first concerts consisted particularly in amusement and even though symphonies or chamber works were played in them they took place in restaurant facilities where wine was served and where the assembled society came chiefly for entertainment while also listening to music. Such concerts were organized in Prague in the Convict, in Platýz palace and in other places. They had a more august character only in theatres (e. g. Nosticz theatre) which were attended by visitors already used to listen to serious music. These productions were performed both by artists from the Italian opera companies and local musicians.

A special chapter of the Czech musical history is formed by the so-called musical emigration. The social, religious and ethnic conditions unfavourable to music prevailing in the Czech lands caused that a lot of Czech musicians left the country in the 18th century to make their living abroad. Some of them left the country only for a short period of time others had never returned. This included even some cruel aspects when warrant was issued for arrest of some musicians, for instance, those from the Prague Count Thun orchestra for unauthorized emigration abroad without consent of their lord. Although the Czech musicians were extraordina-

The Auersperk, formerly Clary palace (No. 16) is located at the corner of Tomášská Street and Valdštejnské square in the Lesser Quarter. Comtesse Josephine Clary was an excellent singer and mandolin player. During his Prague stay in 1796 Ludwig van Beethoven wrote compositions for mandolin and harpsichord for her. The outstanding personality of the musical life of Prague of that time and an excellent pedagogue Wenceslas John Tomášek lived in the neighbouring Kopf house and died here in 1850. He contributed with his piano pieces to the development of the Czech Romantic style

rily gifted people their talents did not have the opportunity to develop in such a manner so as to grow into artists who would provide the high Classicism in music with their own character and nature. Despite this fact we cannot imagine the development of the musical Classicism without their creative contribution. This applies, in particular, to the composers John Wenceslas Stamic (1717–1757), Joseph Mysliveček (1737–1781), Francis Benda (1709–1786), John Zach (1699–1773), George Anthony Benda (1722–1795), Adalbert Jírovec (1763–1850), John Bapitst Vaňhal (1739–1813), Wenceslas Pichl (1741–1805), Anthony Rejcha (1770–1836), Leopold Koželuh (1747–1818), John Wenceslas Voříšek (1791–1825), Paul (1756–1808) and Anthony (1761–1820) Vranický and many others. Their works were spread and played throughout the whole of Europe. They did not live or work in their homeland – or only for a short period of time – so that nobody of them could grow into the greatness and immortality of Haydn, Mozart or Beethoven particularly as a result of the fact that none of them managed to produce an unparalleled synthesis of the Classicism which was an extraordinarily vivid style.

However, a number of authors stayed in Prague and took a substantial part in the development of the local musical life. These creative personalities included, for instance, Francis Xaver Brixi (1732–1771) who studied music in the Piarist college in Kosmonosy and later worked successfully in Prague cathedrals as organ player and composer. As a young man in the age of twenty-seven he became the conductor of the metropolitan St. Vitus's cathedral. Although he did not live up to forty years of his age he produced more than 500 works performed not only in Prague but also in Poland, Austria and Germany. These included cathedral works of all kinds – big passion oratorios, festive masses with huge musical apparatus, etc. He was the type of composer standing out by a perfect counterpoint technique and, therefore, we can say that his work is a skilful combination of the Baroque music technique with the musical elements of the early Classicism. Another significant Prague author Francis Xaver Dušek (1730–1799) became – due to his education and wide musical overview – one of the main musical advisors in aristocratic families. His piano pieces, in particular, have an extraordinary standard maintaining their vitality up to our days. John Anthony Koželuh (1738–1814) became the conductor in St. Vitus's cathedral where his sacred works were performed as well. He contributed substantially also to the history of the Prague opera music by his two operas composed in the "Italian" spirit – operas Alessandro nell India

(Alexander the Great in India, 1760) and Demofoonte (1772) – which were successfully played in Nosticz (the Estates) theatre. John August Vitásek (1770–1839) was a great admirer of Mozart's music. He composed his works in Mozart's style and his importance for the Prague musical life consisted in that he became the successor of J. A. Koželuh in St. Vitus's cathedral.

Unquestionably, one of the most important musical personalities of the musical Prague of the late 18th century and the first half of the following century was Wenceslas John Tomášek (1770–1850). He had a tremendous social influence not only among musicians but also in the environment of prominent noble families. Soon he became domestic composer of Count J. F. Buquoy. He was an excellent but a little conservative musical pedagogue, too. Hence, his name is connected with his famous students, such as the already mentioned John Wenceslas Voříšek, Alexander Dreyschok (1818–1869), John Frederic Kittl (1806–1868), Eduard Hanslick (1825–1904) and many others. Many of them learnt music in Prague but then developed their talents in full only abroad. For his extraordinary influence V. J. Tomášek was called ironically "the Prague musical Pope" which, however, represented no obstacles for such personalities as Niccolo Paganini (1782–1840), Richard Wagner (1813–1883) and Hector Berlioz (1803–1869) to come to greet him during their Prague visits and make a bow. From among Tomášek's works created in Prague his piano pieces, such as Eclogues, Rhapsodies, Dithyrambs are considered outstanding as well as works of greater size of the type of Missa solemnis (Solemn mass). Tomášek is said that by his artistic asset he became a sort of a connecting link between the Czech Classicism and the work of Bedřich Smetana belonging already to the nationalist-marked style period.

When looking back at the musical life of Prague in the period of the Classicism when Bohemia with Prague at the head was generally regarded as a sort of a musical conservatoire of Europe we can only say with regret that it was chiefly external circumstances that made it impossible that Prague with its human artistic potential would play a crucial role in the development of the then European music. A full development of the national musical culture in all its important forms and types was not possible at that time. Similarly, this Central European metropolis was not able to create favourable conditions for the occurrence of a really national opera, such as in Italy, Austria, France and elsewhere. Prague had to wait for the creation of a virtually national musical style several more decades and only then the needed circumstances matured in the sphere of the nationalist-marked social consciousness.

The whole west side of Malostranské square is occupied by the front of the Liechtenstein palace in the entirely Classicist style after the reconstruction made by the architect Matthew Hummel in 1791. Domestic concerts and balls were organized also in this palace. Music was provided by the artists from the Italian operetta companies as well as by domestic musicians. Today the palace is the residence of the musical department of the Academy of Performing Arts and concerts of the students are held here

In the period of Romanticism

The memorial plate with the bust of Ludwig van Beethoven at the wall of the house No. 285 in Lázeňská Street in the Lesser Quarter by Otakar Španiel commemorates one of the stays of this musical giant in Prague in 1796. The house of the Golden Unicorn ("U Zlatého jednorožce"), a hotel at that time, had another significant guest in the field of music – Charles Burney, the author of the Musical Travel of the 18th century lived here in 1772

The period of the early Romanticism in the Czech music coincides with the period of the Czech national revival. Tough centralism imposed in the Czech lands already in the times of the reforms of the Empress Maria Theresa and her son Joseph II by the Vienna government led to a strengthened Germanization which showed itself adversely especially in Prague – in the administrative, bureaucratic and cultural fields. The nation defended itself not only by means of its cultural intelligentsia but also by the influence of the Czech country which did not reconcile itself with the fact that its own mother tongue would be forgotten.

Also music played a positive role in this process even though the Czech composers in this period had not achieved top artistic performance. They had pre-

One of Prague's oldest Gothic temples, the church of St. Gallus in the White Friar monastery was reconstructed in the Baroque style at the beginning of the 18th century. The interior of the church contains remarkable works of the foremost Baroque painters and sculptors. Like other foremost Prague temples, this church has maintained an intensive musical life. Here, compositions a cappella and vocal instrumental works could be heard at an exceptionally artistic standard performed with magnificent grandiosity

ECCE EGO MITTAM VOBIS

pared, however, development prerequisites which later, in the period of the Neo-Romanticism bore fruit in the form of a nationally distinct, worldwide acknowledged musical culture.

In the period of the early Romanticism musical creative work was leaving the original elements of the Classicism apprehended as common style hallmarks providing the artists with creative freedom, real assertion of individuality and artistic imagination drawing from emotionally coloured subjective experiences. While the preceding periods of the Baroque and Classicism produced music without dependence on literary ideas (mainly instrumental music in various chamber and orchestra instruments), music of the Romantic era was returning to a union with extra-musical phenomena and poetical ideas to achieve finally a higher development type of the so-called programme music. This fact disrupted the schemes of classical musical forms, disturbed the symmetry of melodiousness as well as the clear harmony order. Suddenly, musical expression became an exclusive, individually distinct artistic matter. Typical artist, a titan of musical production from the turn of the 18th and 19th centuries was Ludwig van Beethoven. He represented the climax of the musical Classicism but, at the same time, opened the path for a new musical style by the connection of his music with generally established ideas.

However, Prague at the beginning of the 19th century was captured for a long time by the cult of Mozart which, on the one hand, was a beneficial incentive for the artists to work intensively but, on the other hand, disabled understanding of an artistic stream of a new character. This was also the reason why for many decades Beethoven was accepted in Prague with lesser interest than as his significance and importance of his works would deserve. The rare Prague performances of his Eroica in 1807 and the Pastoral symphony four years later conducted by Friedrich D. Weber (1766–1842) as well as the performance of his opera Fidelio in 1814 in the Estates Theatre conducted by Carl Maria von Weber (1786–1826) were exceptions only. Similarly, one of the first concerts of Beethoven's works in Prague was performed only upon external impetus in 1839 to support money collection for the building of the composer's memorial in Bonn. So, it was only in 1856 that Prague could hear for the first time Beethoven's festive mass Missa solemnis as one of the top works of the author. Czech composers living in Prague did not respond to Beethoven's work (an exception was only John Wenceslas Voříšek in Vienna) by which to a certain degree they prevented the advent of an independent, original Czech Romanticism. Despite this fact it cannot be said that Prague was disdainful in relation to new trends in music, but it accepted them as a foreign art, mainly as interesting inspiration from abroad and not as something to be absorbed in a creative manner. For instance, in 1816 the excellent composer and conductor Carl Maria von Weber presented Spohr's opera Faust in the Estates Theatre, Joseph Triebensee produced Weber's opera The Freischütz in 1822 and Marschner's The Vampire in 1829. In the same theatre there were performances of operas of Romantic type: Auber's The Mute from Portici (Masaniello) (1829), Rossini's William Tell (1830) and Meyerbeer's Robert the Devil (1835). But it was only the Czech composer and conductor of the Estates Theatre Francis Škroup (1801–1862) who later took credit for introducing to the Prague stage operas of excellent standard – Verdi's Nabucodonosor and Ernani (1849), Rigoletto (182), Il Trovatore (1856). In this theatre, soon after their creation the first operas of Richard Wagner were presented: Tannhäuser (1854), Lohengrin (1856), The Flying Dutchman (1856) and Rienzi (1859) by

According to older tradition, the synagogue called Old School in Dušní Street in the Old Town was considered to be the oldest synagogue in Prague. Reformed divine service was introduced in the Old School in 1837 a part of which is synagogue music. In 1836–1845 musical life was provided here by Francis Škroup, the creator of the Czech national anthem, and his brother John Nepomuk Škroup worked here as the choir-leader. The synagogue of today – now called the Spanish synagogue – was built at the place of the former Old School in 1882–1893 in a pseudo-oriental form according to the project of the architect Joseph Niklas

The edifice of the Dominican monastery with St. Giles's church in the Old Town. In about 1730 the originally Gothic temple was reconstructed in the Baroque style according to the plans by Francis Špaček and Francis Maxmilian Kaňka while the interior was decorated with frescos by Wenceslas Laurel Reiner. The building of the monastery became in 1811 the first residence of the Prague conservatoire which gave education to a number of excellent musicians. World renown was acquired, for instance, by the excellent violin player Joseph Slavík or the singer Henrietta Sontagová

which Prague as a significant centre of Wagnerianism surpassed Vienna and Leipzig.

In the spirit of the revivalist efforts as well as by gradual taking over of the initiative by the bourgeois circles from the hands of nobility, new institutions were being established also in the field of culture becoming the bearers of musical progress for the whole 19th century. In 1803 the Tonkünstler-Sozietät (Society of Musical Artists) was founded in Prague as a self-help institution for the support of widows and orphans of past musicians. The positive feature of this activity was that this society acquired financial funds from the receipts of oratorio and soloist concerts. Initially these productions were German but from the 1860s concerts with works of German and Czech origin alternated. The society carried out this exceptionally noble-hearted mission for a hundred years.

The coffer ceiling of the grand hall at the isle of Žofín was painted by Francis Duchoslav and the four figural inlays were produced by Victor Oliva. This wonderful environment was the place of balls, popular concerts, the so-called Artistic Debates (Umělecká beseda), and the first Czech symphonic concerts in Prague. The isle of Žofín lives its social life even today. Here is a production of the joint choirs and the symphonic orchestra of the Basic School of Arts of Prague 5

Another important society founded in 1810 in Prague by the Prague aristocrats was the Verein zur Beförderung der Tonkunst in Böhmen (Union for the Improvement of Church Music in Bohemia). The foremost supporters of its included also Count Pachta. The union was aware that without ensuring education of quality musicians from among the local young talented generation the development of music in Prague or elsewhere in Bohemia could not achieve a more significant bloom. For this reason it initiated the establishment of the conservatoire in 1811. This was a blessed deed for the development of music in Prague. The newly established institute not only educated new, exceptional quality musicians but it also took care for a systematic concert life in Prague. It did not last long and the Prague conservatoire became a famous school of a high artistic and pedagogical standard. It was connected with the renowned violin school of Wilhelm Pixis (1786–1842), violoncello school of Bernard Wenceslas Šťastný (about 1760–1835) as well as with the contrabass school of Wenceslas House (1764–1847) and many others. Excellent results were achieved by the Prague conservatoire also in the field of woodwind instruments. This renown of the institute which in no time exceeded even the borders of the homeland caused that Prague became a favourite place for visits by the world's foremost artists. These included the Italian wonder violinist Niccolo Paganini, the German violinist Ludwig Spohr (1784–1859), the French violinist Jacques Mazas (1782–1849), the Belgian virtuosos Henri Vieuxtemps (1820–1881) and Charles de Bériot (1802–1870), the Norwegian violinist Ole Bull (1810–1880), the pianists Franz Liszt (1811–1886), Clara Schumann (1819–1896), Anton Grigorievich Rubinstein (1829–1894), Hans von Bülow (1830–1894) and others. Many of them were also composers and presented their works in Prague.

Another society striving for a revival of the cultural life in Prague was the bilingual Verein für Kunstfreude für Kirchenmusik in Bömen (Union for Church Music in Bohemia) established in 1826 which built gradually the Institute for Education of Organists and Choir Directors in Prague or the so-called organist school. In 1871 studies in this school were extended from two years to three years and in 1891 it was merged with the Prague music conservatoire.

In 1840 the sing and music society Caecilienverlein (Cecilian Unity) started its twenty-five-years activity in Prague. Its main domain was producing concerts. The Prager Singakademie (Academy for Improvement of Singing and Music in Prague) had similar targets. It was also known under the name of the Žofín Academy (Žofínská akademie). These societies took part in dozens of concerts with oratorio, cantata and choir works. The academy instigated also the creation of new works by declaring creative tender competitions. The main merit, however, was that they brought up the Prague audience toward listening of classical music until the end of the 19th century when they were replaced by institutions of another, more modern type. Even though these two societies competed with each other in the field of their repertoire and struggled for popularity with the Prague audience they took credit, in particular, for the production of the principal works by Johann Sebastian Bach and Georg Friedrich Händel in Prague and, moreover, for the timely learning of the supreme works of the German Romanticists, namely the works by Felix Mendelssohn-Bartholdy (1809–1847) and Robert Schumann (1810–1856). The Žofín Academy even ventured to perform Beethoven's Symphony No. 9.

Beside this progress in the field of public concerts in the first half of the 19th century Prague maintained a very intensive musical life in the foremost churches

Already in 1837 in the Slavonic isle (Slovanský ostrov), then called Žofín, there was a building which was a place of significant events of the Czech social and political life. The building of today is a result of an extension in 1886 and Neo-Renaissance reconstruction. The isle of Žofín which is in close vicinity of the National Theatre is connected with the tradition of big Czech balls and concerts where concerts were made also by such artists as Franz Liszt and Hector Berlioz

and cathedrals, such as St. Vitus's cathedral, the churches of St. Nicholas, St. James, St. Gallus, St. Stephan, Knights of the Cross and others. Here, works a capella as well as vast vocal and instrumental works could be heard at an extraordinary artistic level with grandiose magnificence. In the period before March 1848 when nobility salons still existed in Prague (such as those of John Nosticz, Francis Šternberk, Christian Clam-Gallas, J. F. Buquoy, Francis Kinský, Joseph Nosticz and Countess Ellis Šlik) these salons, on the one hand, were opened to new streams in art and invited the on-coming generation of Czech artists and, on the other hand, they became a model for music cultivation in bourgeois households.
Unfortunately, the situation within the pre-March absolutism of Metternich as well as the post-March one of Bach were not favourable for such a music production in homes. In poorer homes people played the guitar and sang while in the richer families piano playing dominated. Prague was still far away from such a situation when a real bourgeois salon would be established for which a new, valuable works would be created. It was not only a period of a tough absolutist centralism but also of police informer spying when any a little bit more liberal or non-conform expression was considered an anti-Hapsburg intention.

An increase in attractiveness of the musical life in the revivalist but politically still humiliated Prague was contributed greatly by visits of significant foreign artists – the first representatives of the Romanticism in the European music. Beside the author of The Freischütz C. M. Weber and young Richard Wagner whose works were presented in the Estates Theatre, these included, in particular, Hector Berlioz (1803–1869) who by his six concerts in the palace at the isle of Žofín in 1846 managed to disturb the peaceful level of musical activities in Prague. He conducted his works, such as overture King Lear, The Fantastic Symphony, The Carnival in Rome, Harold in Italy and others which brought a new type of Romantic and programme music in the field of orchestral music. Prague was enthused by Berlioz's works in the same manner as their author was enchanted by the beauty of the city and the musical feeling of its inhabitants. Ten year later Prague was visited by Franz Liszt who until then was considered to be a representative of the German Romantic rather than Hungarian national music. With extraordinary success he conducted his Esztergom Mass in St. Vitus's cathedral. He came to Prague again in 1858 but now with his programme music works of the type of the Dante Symphony and symphonic poems Tasso and Ideals. On this occasion he also performed brilliantly his two famous piano concertos.

Prague in the first half of the 19th century did not lose contact with the world in the field of performance art. This, however, does not apply to the field of creative composing work. Although the local authors, such as J. B. Kittl (1806–1868), Wenceslas Henry Veit (1806–1864), Anthony Emil Titl (1809–1882), Francis Škroup (1801–1862) and his brother John Nepomuk Škroup (1811–1892) composed works of all musical types none of them achieved a standard comparable with the works of the musical Romanticists abroad. Even though the operas by František Škroup Dráteník (The Tinker, 1826), Oldřich and Božena (1828), Fidlovačka (Shoemakers' Spring Festival, 1834) and Libušin sňatek (The Marriage of Libuše, 1835) are significant as an evidence of the existence of the first Czech opera works of the early Romanticism (the national anthem of the later Czech state "Kde domov můj" – "Where Is My Home" – has its origin in the opera Fidlovačka with text by Joseph Kajetán Tyl) they had no significant influence on the later development of the Czech national music. A certain exception from among the composers living in Prague was the already mentioned work by V.J. Tomášek who, however, due to his enthusiastic admiration of the work of Mozart – and more or less rejecting attitude to the work of Beethoven – ultimately stagnated at the border between the Classicism and Romanticism.

This disproportion between the world music and the work of the local composers, especially in the first half of the 19th century (at the beginning of the 1860s) was surely influenced by the position of Prague within the framework of the European metropolises. Prague was a provincial, politically insignificant city only slowly getting rid of the load of the Germanizing trends which according to the predestination of the Hapsburgs should quell it as a nation. It only started to fight for its Czech identity. It was a slow process. First, it asserted itself in the field of folk songs, folk and social dances, and later also by composing the so-called patriotic songs. After the abolishment of serfdom in Bohemia in 1781 under the rule of Joseph II (1780–1790) lots of country people come to Prague with their songs and dances which are fervently learnt, sung and danced by the inhabitants of Prague. The preciousness of this treasury of national culture was understood particularly by the collectors of these gems of folklore, such as John Jeník of Bratřice (1756–1845), John Ritter of Ritterberk (1778–1841), Francis Ladislav Čelakovský (1799–1852), Charles Jaromír Erben (1811–1870), Francis Sušil (1804–1868) and others. In the field of dancing, the popularity of polka was so great that it pushed out from the dancing halls a great number of original folk dances ("obkročák", "skočná", "sousedská", "hulán", "medvěd" and others) and became the most characteristic cultural and social expression of the Czech society in the 19th century. For instance, polka "Esmeralda" of 1838 by Francis Matthew Hilmera (1803–1881) was played at all Czech balls. It served as a model for almost all composers of both the young and older generations when composing polka dancing works. As a typical expression of the Czech national life polka passed later into the artificial, high stylized work of the composers Bedřich Smetana (1824–1884), Antonín Dvořák (1841–1904) as well as other authors.

In the period of Neo-Romanticism

In 1910–1911 so-called trigas – bronze statues of three horses with the goddesses of Victory were mounted on the pylons of the main front of the National Theatre. The trigas are the decoration of the building increasing its impressiveness. The production of the sculpture was participated by Bohuslav Schnirch and his pupils Francis Rous, Emanuel Halman and Ladislav Šaloun, the master the Prague Art Nouveau who endowed the whole work with its dynamism

The National Theatre belongs by its style perfection, architectonic beauty, layout disposition and ingenious mastery to the peaks of the Czech architecture of the 19th century. The construction is connected with the names of the architects Joseph Zítek and Joseph Schulz and a whole range of Czech artists who took part in the decoration of its exterior and interior

The period from 1860 to approximately the 1890s is one of the most important parts of the modern Czech history when the emancipation process of the Czech society came to its climax. It made such a progress that during that period the Czech science, culture and art came to the same level as the advanced European nations. This process was significant and it was no chain of coincidences. By the abolishment of Bach's absolutism and adoption of the so-called October diploma in 1860 the Austrian Emperor Francis Joseph I who headed the Hapsburg dynasty for 68 years (1848–1916) undertook to adopt a constitution on the basis of which the Czech lands would regain a dignified political position in the Hapsburg multinational confederation of states. Already by the fact that

Bohemia had again its representation in the imperial assembly justifying many hopes created the prerequisite for the development of a national life in all the strata of the Czech society. The October diploma, however, was no final victory. It only opened slightly the door for the opportunities for trying to fulfil itself in all the fields of activities which were so important for it. Prague, its intelligentsia as well as the enthusiasm of the widest social strata of its inhabitants for everything connected with the tradition of the Czech nation, from singing songs to patriotic balls, from studies of own history to establishing new artistic and scientific societies, played a decisive role in this process. It became a model also for the other towns of Bohemia and Moravia.

In the periods until 1860 social life was developing in bilingual connection of the Czech and German cultures but after 1860 this situation changed all of a sudden. The separation of the two cultures, particularly in Prague was definitive. In many cases there was mutual ignoring as well as combative clashes of the nationally different communities. This also led to a dissolution or split of the hitherto German-Czech musical institutions.

Art as the first phenomenon of all the fields of national life tried to get out from the provincial position within the framework of the Austrian-Hungarian monarchy. Both in the institutional area and in the artistic and creative area it was striving to be incorporated into the

The lobby of the National Theatre is decorated with fourteen lunette pictures by Mikoláš Aleš from 1878 depicting the topic of homeland and four wall paintings by Mikoláš Aleš and František Ženíšek. The ceiling bears the triptych Decline, Resurrection and The Golden Age of Arts by František Ženíšek. In the lobby there is the allegorical statue of Music by Josef Václav Myslbek and the busts of the personalities who contributed to the development of the theatre produced by other sculptors

The curtain of the National Theatre is the work of the painter Vojtěch Hynais. The author designed it in such a way so that it would be a celebration of the construction of the National Theatre. The painting depicts the artists, workers and all who participated in the construction as well as a number of specific details of that time: a poor woman sacrificing a gift for the theatre and a skinflint. Hynais's painting was a vanguard work in its time. The inscription above the curtain bears the idea of the theatre which was created thanks to all-national collections of money "The People for Themselves"

European or world stream of musical life. It was no mere coincidence that the Czech artists of that period earned the name "the generation of the National Theatre". This was because the idea of the establishment and existence of the nation's own theatre where the Czech people would fulfil themselves in a creative manner, hence, giving a clear evidence to the world about the peculiarity and maturity of the Czech nation, was an idea supported with enthusiasm not only by politicians, scientists, architects, men of letters and artists of all fields but also by citizens of various social strata. Prague and the country were at one in this process although the main forces for the establishment of the most significant national values were ripening in the metropolis of Prague.

The lobby of the National Theatre – ceiling decorated according to the cartoons by František Ženíšek. The central part of the triptych with the main figure of the Homeland – Czechia with her son Nation. The lunnets in the lobby are made according to the Czech painter Mikoláš Aleš

The nature of the Neo-Romanticism in music was not only a deeper bond of music with literature, poetry, national ideas and myths but also individual differentiation of the musical expression of individual composer personalities. The musical styles of the Baroque and Classicism were characterized by uniform features of musical expression which were disturbed substantially already by Beethoven and the first Romanticists. This trend of the early Romanticism was not changed by the Neo-Romanticism but was strengthened and put to a head. It was connected directly also with the creation of national art. The artists were looking for sources for the expression of the national character of their musical works not by imitating folk songs, their melodies and simple dance rhythms but by incorporating all their characteristic features into the individual composition process. They emphasized the significance of the word and music declamation for the creation of the nationally viewed melodious part of music, they strove for monumentality (in operas, symphonic poems, cantatas and oratorios) which would express best the seriousness and greatness of the national ideas. It was also this inclining to national pathos rising from inside that differed the Neo-Romanticism from the more intimate and innermost early Romanticism.

The models for the Czech music authors were, in particular, composers who had already gone through this development – Hector Berlioz, Franz Liszt and Richard Wagner. They gave their art completely to the service of the Neo-Romantic ideas which was appreciated by Prague not only through increased attention toward their works but also during their artistic visits. But it was not unilateral. These models included also artists of seemingly antagonist orientation – Johannes Brahms (1833–1897) respecting especially in the field of the so-called absolute music as obligatory the classicizing tradition and perfection of the formal structure of music, and Giuseppe Verdi (1813–1901), the opposite to Wagner, not relinquishing the aria conception of musical melodiousness and traditional structure of musical drama. Although there were frequent sharp disputes between the supporters of these two types of musical creation they did not weaken the awareness of the exceptional artistic asset of these worldwide acknowledged celebrities. Even Prague was not spared the passionate polemics concerning the true nature of the Neo-Romantic, i. e. modern national art. In some respects these different attitudes – demonstrated later in even quarrelsome assessment of the personalities of Smetana and Dvořák – have survived in the view of the music of our classics up to our days.

The advance of the Czech music after 1860 was assisted by the establishing of music societies, namely choirs which livened up the bustle and pathos of the national life in a social manner in Prague and elsewhere. First, only men societies were founded, later also women and mixed ones. In the field of physical culture a tremendous role was played by the sports association "Sokol". A similar role in the field of singing was played by the Prague society "Hlahol" founded in 1861 under the slogan "Through singing to the heart, through the heart to the homeland". Active part in the activities of this significant society was played also by

Decoration of the ceiling of the National Theatre. Eight allegorical paintings – Lyrics, Epics, Dance, Mimics, Sculpture, Architecture, Painting, and Music – according to the cartoons by František Ženíšek – crowning the fillings of the centre of the auditorium ceiling

the composers Bedřich Smetana (he conducted Hlahol in 1863–1865), Charles Bendl (1838–1897) and others. The significance of the Prague Hlahol was not only in the fact that it became a model for massive establishing of singer societies throughout Bohemia and Moravia (there were over 250 of them by the end of the 1860s) but also the fact that its choir performance was at an extraordinary high level. Hlahol participated in productions of such significant vocal and instrumental works as Beethoven's Missa solemnis, Berlioz's Requiem, Liszt's oratorium Christ, Dvořák's Stabat mater and cantata Wedding Shirt, etc. It initiated to a great degree also the creation of a new choir literature a cappella which by its originality, technical maturity and artistic value (e. g. Bedřich Smetana's works Dowry, Peasant's Song, Song of the Sea, Three Riders, Renegade and others) became to a certain degree a worldwide acknowledged value with which the Czech choirs won international recognition especially from the beginning of the 20th century.

The building called "Malý Platýz" No. 415 opposite the St. Martin's church bears the bust of the world known composer Franz Liszt to the memory of his concerts here in 1840 and 1846. The author belonged to the founders of the Neo-Romantic music, visited Prague several times and interpreted his piano pieces and orchestral works – for instance, in 1856 he conducted his Esztergom Mass in St. Vitus's cathedral

Values complying with the Neo-Romantic bond of literary idea with music were created also in the field of symphonic music. The supreme creative work in this spirit was Smetana's uniquely designed cycle of symphonic poems My Country which in its whole and formal shape is a unique work of art in worldwide terms. In this work the author expressed by merely musical means not only the famous past of the Czech nation (in the poems Vyšehrad, Šárka, Tábor) but also the beauty of the Czech land and its nature (The Vltava, From Bohemia's Fields and Groves) and the future vision of an independent existence of the Czech nation (Blaník). After Smetana it was only Antonín Dvořák – instigated by Brahms – who created the Czech type of symphony (e. g. with "swaggerer's" dancing rhythms in scherzo of the Symphony No. 6). From among his nine symphonies, the last one, composed in the United States and called From the New World is the

The sculpture depicting Ferdinand Laub (1832–1875) in the Seminary garden at the hill of Petřín is the work of Vojtěch Sapík. It reminds us of the brilliant Czech violinist whose mastery was highly appreciated even by the world composers Hector Berlioz or Peter Ilyich Chaikovsky. The tombstone of Ferdinand Laub can be found at the Vyšehrad cemetery beside other famous Czech artists

most famed. Dvořák, however, was also the creator of the Czech oratorios and cantatas (Stabat mater, Wedding Shirt, St. Ludmilla, Requiem, Te Deum, etc.) which contributed substantially to the fame of the Czech music in the world.

Like in the case of the choir movement which found its mass base in the ideas of the development of the national life, the Czech society of the 1860s escalated its endeavour also in the activities connected with the establishment of the Czech theatre. The Estates Theatre which was renamed in 1861 to Royal Land Theatre in Prague gave plays in Czech only on Sunday afternoons which was insufficient and undignified for the awakened nationalist efforts of the Czech patriots. In a short period of several months it was proven unrealistic to start to build a big theatre as a definite expression of the modern artistic efforts of the Czech people. Therefore, in 1862 a small theatre called the Provisional Theatre was built at the Vltava embankment. The original prognoses that this theatre will serve to the Czech art only three years evolved into a provisional state lasting no less than twenty years. Despite the lack of room in this theatre (auditorium had only 151 seats, 140 standing places, 39 boxes and two galleries for 500 persons) where even the fully filled orchestra lacked space, this theatre fulfilled its historical purpose. It played four times a week. Opera was played once a week with the help of the orchestra of Charles Komzák which after supplementing further musicians (with total number of 34 instrumentalists only) fulfilled the function of the theatre orchestra. The first conductor of the Provisional Theatre was John Nepomuk Maýr (1818–1888), efficient musician and organizer, former opera singer with substantial theatre experience but a routinist without deeper artistic ambitions. For the years 1866–1874 he was replaced by Bedřich Smetana which, however, could not make do without passionate disputes in the Prague press. As conductor and later chief of opera Smetana endowed the theatre with a number of high targets which were to become obligatory in the future for the artistic endeavour in this field as such. These included a progressive repertoire from the West European music (Gluck, Gounod, Mozart, Beethoven, etc.) as well as support to Slavonic composers (Glinka, Moniuszko, etc.) but, in particular, systematic presentation of original Czech works, too. Premiers of all significant operas of the domestic repertoire took place in this theatre – Smetana's The Brandenburgers in Bohemia, The Bartered Bride, The Two Widows, The Kiss, The Secret; Šebor's The Templars in Moravia, Drahomíra, The Hussite Bride, Blanka; Rozkošný's Nicholas and St. John's Streams; Blodek's In the Well; Hřímalý's The Enchanted Prince; Bendl's The Old Bridegroom; and the first operas by Dvořák The King and the Collier, Vanda, The Pigheaded Peasants, and The Peasant a Rogue. The theatre played a positive role also in the field of education of excellent operatic singers and, in particular, education of the Prague opera audience which later became an important background for the existence and activity of the future National Theatre. The small and insufficiently equipped building of the so-called Provisional Theatre was in the end included as the rear tract into the premises of the new theatre building admired by the entire nation.

The memorial plate with a bust at the wall of the house No. 14 in Žitná Street made by Otakar Španiel in 1927 reminds us that this was the place of living of the Czech composer Antonín Dvořák, the Czech composer of Neo-Romantic music and its worldwide established representative. He was famous as an excellent pedagogue in his homeland as well as in the United States who educated a whole generation of musical composers

The most famous domestic operas staged in the Provisional Theatre included, in particular, the operas by Bedřich Smetana. Already the first work of his, The Brandenburgers in Bohemia (premiere 5 Janury, 1866) was welcomed with enthusiasm by the Prague audience and the Czech musical and literary critics as a real product of the Czech national output. The case of The Bartered Bride was more difficult. Although its premiere followed shortly after The Brandenburgers (30 May, 1866) it was no big success. Prague was threatened by a short-time invasion by the Prussian army and so people were running away and were not interested in theatre. Only during repeated performances and especially after the author's re-making of the opera (from the original two acts now there

The Michna Baroque summer palace called America has served since 1932 as Antonín Dvořák Museum with an exhibition of his life and work with concerts of his music. The author was honoured as one of the greatest geniuses especially in England and the United States. The members of the Original Musical Theatre Prague are performing Dvořák's most beautiful arias in the hall with the original wall paintings

were three acts and its prose was changed into composed recitatives) The Bartered Bride became the highest national and most frequently played Czech opera of all. When the Provisional Theatre ended its activity in 1881 it had already its 110th performance which was something unprecedented in the case of a Czech opera. And it was this work that many years later, in 1892 at the International Theatre and Music Exhibition in Vienna where it was performed by the Prague National Theatre, met with an extraordinary response which broke the hitherto isolation or absence of the Czech musical and dramatic works at the world's stages.

Four years after the Provisional Theatre was established trying in straitened circumstances to provide the people with what was missing up to that time so much, Prague witnessed a new marvellous event: festive laying down of the foundation stone for the building of the National Theatre. This stone was brought from the hill of Říp in a 30 kilometre's distance from Prague. This hill is connected with the myth about the settlement of the Czech people in this country. It was laid down in the future space of the theatre with assistance and speeches of all significant personalities of the Prague cultural life, including the historian Francis Palacký (1798–1876), the leading politician Francis Ladislav Rieger (1818–1903) as well as Bedřich Smetana. A part of this festive event held on 16 May 1868 was the performance of

Smetana's choir Peasant's Song and the first performance of Smetana's opera Dalibor in the New Town Theatre.

A peculiarity of the building of the National Theatre was the fact that it was built up from money collections of the Czech people, all the social strata, from the poorest to the wealthiest. Even the simplest peasant cottagers in the foothill villages voluntarily contributed – be it by a couple of coins only – since even they were interested in the building of a theatre which would symbolize and express in the future the desire of the Czech nation for its re-incorporation into the family of the advanced nations of Europe. The collections took place under the slogan "The People for Themselves". Therefore the builders of the theatre placed these worlds above the curtain painted by the artist Hynais. It is also due to this fact that the building became a rarity in the history of opera houses in the whole of Europe. The theatre was built according to the plans of the architect Josef Zítek (1832–1909) but its decoration was participated by countless artists, mainly sculptors and painters. Even musicians and dramatic artists were not standing aside creating purposefully musical and dramatic works for their staging in the newly constructed theatre. Bedřich Smetana composed opera Libuše for the opening of the activity of the theatre and for other festive occasions even though it had to last no less than 9 years from its accomplishment that it had its premiere on 11 June, 1881. But the original National Theatre played nine days only. A huge fire destroyed everything almost to the grounds. Based on the first shock which stroke painfully the whole Czech patriotic public, in no time new collections were organized with unexpected spontaneity and selflessness which brought in more than a million guilders. Hence, the inscription above the curtain "The People for Themselves" became a real symbol of the tabernacle of arts, the Golden Chapel above the Vltava as the people started to call it by which

The originally Baroque summer palace called Portheimka built in 1725 by Kilian Ignaz Dienzenhofer hosted in the time when it was possessed by the arts favourer Joseph Portheim a number of artists, including Antonín Dvořák. In 1876, upon Portheim's initiative, the Union for Chamber Music in Prague was established and its concerts were participated by Zdeněk Fibich, Francis Ondříček and many others. Here also the first performance of the Czech Quartet took place

the nation made all the world aware of its determined will to have its national identity. The new theatre – in which now, preventively, no wood was used – was re-built under the control of the architect Josef Schulz in the shortest possible time (in 29 months from its burning) and its operation started on 18 November, 1883 again by the festive performance of Smetana's Libuše. By its monumentality and artistic decoration the building overcame all expectations. Its decoration was participated by the sculptors Antonín Wagner (1834–1895), Josef Václav Myslbek (1848–1922), Bohumil Schnirch (1845–1901), the painters Mikoláš Aleš (1852–1913), František Ženíšek (1849–1916), Josef Tulka (1846–1882), Václav Brožík (1851–1901), Adolf Liebscher (1857–1919), Vojtěch Hynais (1854–1925) and Julius Mařák (1832–1899). The generation of the artists of the National Theatre along with the musical and literary authors, actors and operatic singers who were fulfilling its mission became the most energetic and artistically strongest generation inseparably connected with the forming of the Czech national art.

Hybernská Street opposite the ancient Power Gate (Prašná brána) leading to the Old Town of Prague. Here, at the place of the present Neo-Renaissance houses No. 997 and 998 used to be the Saxon Court hotel where Peter Ilyich Chaikovsky lived during his stay in Prague. Here he was often visited by Czech artists, including Antonín Dvořák

The theatre was wonderful, noble and dignified. Almost every citizen no matter from where he came wanted to see it and be present at a performance. Therefore, in the first decade after its opening, there was a well-proven practise of the so-called theatre trains bringing to these performances audience from various places of

Bohemia, from near and distant country locations. Prague was living a rich national life.

Despite this fact and despite the selflessness and significance of the merits of the generation of artists connected with the National Theatre there came a period (especially until 1900 under the director and dramatist František A. Šubert (1849–1915)) when the opera repertoire management was only looking for its true face. The outdated Italian and French works understood as trivial and effective attractions decidedly were not what the Prague audience as well as the other patriotic public expected from this temple of arts. Although this situation was changing gradually already under Šubert's directorship a radical change came only with the advent of the new opera chief Karel Kovařovic at the beginning of the new century.

The front of the Rudolphinum building with a wide entrance stairway dominating square Jana Palacha. The Rudolphinum was built according to the designs by the architects Josef Zítek and Josef Schulz by the architect Václav Vejrych in 1876–1884. The construction was assigned by the Czech Savings Bank (Česká spořitelna) and the edifice should serve to musical and visual arts. The great concert hall is called after Antonín Dvořák who worked here as the conservatoire professor and conductor. An exceptional event was Dvořák's first Prague performance of his Symphony No. 9 in E minor From the New World which the author conducted here on 4 January, 1896

An important institution livening up in an extraordinary manner the cultural life of Prague was the so-called Umělecká beseda (Artistic Debate). It was founded in 1864 specially for the purpose of edifying the Czech art not only in the field of creative work but also in the field of practical cultural activities. It had three sections – musical, visual arts and literary. Its first chairmen were Bedřich Smetana, Josef Mánes (1820–1871) and Vítězslav Hálek (1835–1874). Umělecká beseda made the Czech society aware of itself in the year of its establishment by organizing grandiose festival on the occasion of the 300th anniversary of the birth of William Shakespeare. At the same time, the festival proclaimed the relation of the young Czech art to the tops of the world artistic production and its entry to the world arena. It took place at Prague's greatest stage of the New Town Theatre which had a capacity of 3 thousand visitors. Its dominating feature was a procession of actors and artists in costumes of the characters from the plays of this most famous Renaissance playwright. Bedřich Smetana wrote for this occasion a festive march which is called today Shakespeare march. On this occasion the audience could hear also Berlioz's monumental dramatic symphony Romeo and Juliet with which Prague could get acquainted for the first time when it was conducted by the author in 1846.

The musical section of Umělecká beseda put into life also season-ticket symphonic concerts (in the years 1864–1865) and later a whole series of the so-called popular concerts (since 1869). Unlike Paris, London, Vienna or other European large cities at that time Prague did not had its stable symphonic body. Therefore, the season-ticket and so-called popular concerts had to be performed by musicians from the Czech and German theatres in order that they could take place at all. Here, Umělecká beseda made a virtually extraordinary endeavour. In

A part of the front facade of the Neo-Renaissance edifice of the Rudolphinum. The tall wall of the front with arcade windows, attic and sculptures bears the authorship features of the architect Josef Zítek who built also the National Theatre. The sculptures of lions and sphinxes at the entrance were produced by the sculptor Bohuslav Schnirch while the sitting sculptures are the work by Antonín Wagner. The attic of the building bears statues of significant musical composers and painters

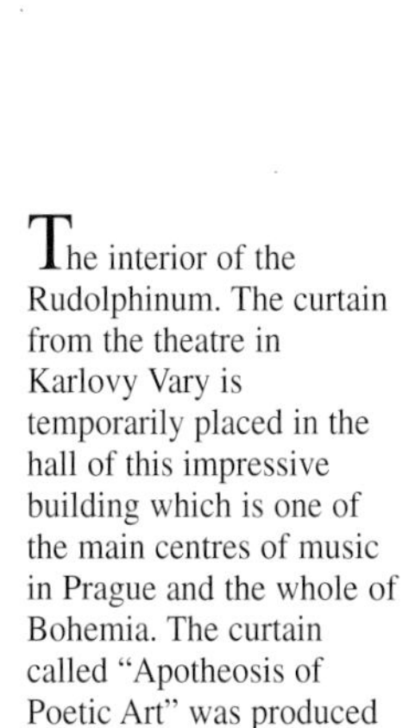

The interior of the Rudolphinum. The curtain from the theatre in Karlovy Vary is temporarily placed in the hall of this impressive building which is one of the main centres of music in Prague and the whole of Bohemia. The curtain called "Apotheosis of Poetic Art" was produced in 1886 by Gustav Klimt, Ernst Klimt and Franz Matsch

particular, the so-called popular concerts presented not only the original production of the Czech authors but also the production of the worldwide acknowledged masters. Moreover, there was a praiseworthy fact that several significant foreign artists were invited to the performance of some concerts.

It was not easy in the then Prague to promote the progressive repertoire management of these concerts whose conductor at the very beginning, before his loss of hearing, was Bedřich Smetana (he conducted a total of 18 concerts). The Neo-Romantic orientation and support of the original domestic works ran into misunderstanding of many influential circles. For instance, the director of the conservatoire Josef Krejčí (1821–1881) expressed his distaste toward any artistic progress by his prohibiting the members of his professor staff to take part in these concerts.

It was an indisputable artistic and social holiday when its concert activities were participated, for instance, by the Hungarian violinist Eduard Reményi who was known, among other things, to take a sharply clear-cut anti-Hapsburg attitude already in the revolutionary year 1848. This artist sent the Prague audience into raptures particularly by his fantasies on Czech folk songs. He was not the only one who met extraordinary response in Prague.

Political resistance of the Czech patriotic circles to the Austrian monarchy for which Prague continued to be a provincial town produced liking to the great and mighty Russia – as a defiance and threat especially after the Austrian-Hungarian political settlement in which the Czech lands were left unjustly rejected. The visits of Peter Ilyich Chaikovsky (1840–1893) in Prague took place in an atmosphere of the excited pro-Russian sentiment. When he came here for the first time on 12 February 1888 he was already at the railway station welcomed by huge crowds of people wanting to express their liking and love for him – not only as an exceptional artist but also as a representative of the Russian people. Then P. I. Chaikovsky loved Prague sincerely. In 1888 he was even twice here. His artistic performances in which he produced for the first time, for instance, his Festive Overture "1812" symbolizing the victory of the Russian people over Napoleon, his later famous Symphony No. 5 in E minor and, in particular, he conducted the Prague premiere of Eugene Onegin in the National Theatre (6 December, 1888) which met with a literally manifestation response. On 10 October, 1892 Chaikovsky took part also in the premiere of The Queen of Spades. During the first two visits in 1888 Chaikovsky was in an almost daily touch with

The stairway of the National Museum occupies almost the whole central wing of the building. Its area under the glass ceiling is decorated with busts of significant personalities and in the corridors are wall pictures of Czech castles. The court walls are decorated with graffiti by Celda Klouček and Josef Fanta. This monumental room is used for concerts

Antonín Dvořák which produced a sincere friendship between them. Antonín Dvořák visited the Russian guest in the hotel "U saského dvora" where the author lived, they jointly went to concerts to the Rudolfinum, Žofín, Měšťanská beseda, etc. Chaikovsky also was a guest of Dvořák's family in their flat at Žitná Street. He also took part in the home banquet held in his honour in the family of the translator of "Onegin" Marie Červinková Riegrová (1854–1895) who was the daughter of the then significant politician František Ladislav Rieger who lived at the present Palackého Street.

In the second half of the 19th century Prague had more than 30 churches where cathedral music was performed. Although the repertoire management of the musical activities in this environment was not too progressive it maintained its standard by productions of classic masses and oratorios by J. Haydn and W. A. Mozart but also of the works by Vitásek and Tomášek. The cathedral choirs were usually headed by perfectly trained local musicians, namely leavers of the Prague organist school. Prague too was affected by the all-European effort for a reform of the church music by returning back to the vocal music by Giovanni Pierluigi da Palestrini (around 1525–1594) and focusing attention on a renaissance of historical musical values. The church of St. Adalbert headed by choir regent Josef Förster (1833–1907) became the centre of this reformed church music in the Prague environment of the 1870s.

The most significant part of the National Museum is the Pantheon – a national sanctuary devoted to the memory of the great personalities of the nation. The square room with galleries has a cupola and the walls are decorated with lunette pictures by František Ženíšek and Václav Brožík. The works are depicting the important events of the Czech history. Moreover, there are bronze statues and busts of the national giants by the greatest Czech sculptors. In the front are busts of Bedřich Smetana and Antonín Dvořák

The charming part of the district of Hradčany – the New World (Nový Svět) – has maintained its picturesque and ancient character. Here, in the house No. 90 is the birthplace of the most famous Czech violinist of the turn of the 19th and 20th centuries František Ondříček (1857–1922) who played an important role, among other things, in the promotion of Dvořák's violin concerto. The house bears a bust by the sculptor Otakar Španiel

It was only after the death of the director of the conservatoire Josef Krejčí in 1881 who managed to isolate the institute from Prague's contemporary concert life that the golden age of the conservatoire activity began. Thanks to the new director Antonín Bennewitz (1833–1926) new excellent artists and musical experts came to this institute, including violin pedagogue Otakar Ševčík (1852–1934), professor of violoncello and chamber play Hanuš Wihan (1855–1920), professor of esthetics and music history Otakar Hostinský (1847–1910) and the world-known composer Antonín Dvořák. All of them – especially after the merger of the conservatoire with the organist school and acquiring of further experienced pedagogues – brought

In the parsonage of St. Adalbert's church in Vojtěšská Street is the memorial of the composer, one of the representatives of Czech modern music Josef Bohuslav Foerster (1859–1951) who was active here. St. Adalbert's church headed by the choir-leader Josef Förster (1833–1907) was the centre of the reformed church music in the 1870s

the institute to an extraordinary level and won it world renown. Although Antonín Bennewitz was German by origin he introduced the Czech language in education and managed to defend the rights of the Czech pedagogues in the institute. Along with his students he created an excellent symphonic orchestra which in the years when there was no professional orchestra body in Prague enriched substantially the concert life in Prague. This orchestra was under Bennewitz's conducting at such a high level that even Antonín Dvořák entrusted it the first "testing" performances of some of his works.

After his loss of hearing in 1874 Bedřich Smetana gradually resigned from all his public activities (conducting, piano activities, organizing concerts and writing to the papers about urging musical problems) and withdrew to seclusion in the countryside. On the other hand, Antonín Dvořák and Zdeněk Fibich (1850–1900) as other two significant representatives of the Neo-Romantic music influenced to a maximum degree the artistic standard of the music in Prague. Dvořák managed this not only by the premieres and frequent symphonic and vocal and orchestral concerts of his works which he conducted himself mainly in the Rudolfinum, a marvellous Neo-Renaissance edifice at the Vltava embankment (today named Alšovo) but also by his fame which accompanied him from abroad (particularly England and the United States honoured him as one of the

The so-called Slavín is the dominant feature of the Vyšehrad cemetery. The joint tomb of the best merited men and women of the Czech nation was projected by the architect Antonín Wiehl and sculptural decoration was created by Josef Mauder. The foremost musical artists and composers are buried throughout the whole Vyšehrad cemetery

greatest contemporary geniuses). Dvořák as a worldwide acknowledged representative of the Czech music was literally loved by the whole Czech nation. His new operas were accepted in Prague with extraordinary enthusiasm. Their premieres were in the National Theatre – namely Jakobin (1888), The Devil and Kate (1897) and The Water Nymph (Rusalka, 1901). Only his last opera Armida staged in the theatre not long before the author's death due to imperfect preparation caused more bitterness than pleasure. In 1891 Dvořák accepted the post of the teacher of composition and instrumentation at the Prague conservatoire and interrupted this work only by his stays in New York. He belonged to excellent pedagogues. By his original manner he educated a whole generation of Czech composers (Josef Suk, Vítězslav Novák, Oskar Nedbal, Julius Fučík, Rudolf Karel to name at least those artistically most distinct) who influenced later the character of the Czech modern (and popular) music. An extraordinary event was Dvořák's first Prague performance of his Symphony No. 9 in E minor From the New World which the author conducted on 4 January, 1896 in the Rudolfinum with an orchestra built by the society called The Czech Philharmonic Orchestra (Česká filharmonie). Although the body proper of the Czech Philharmonic Orchestra was established five years later it is since that moment that the history of this orchestra de facto began. In the next century it played extremely important role in the Prague musical life and made Czech music famous also abroad.

The orchard in the time-honoured Vyšehrad is decorated with the sculptures of Josef Václav Myslbek – Přemysl and Libuše, Záboj and Slavoj, Lumír and Song, and this work Ctirad and Šárka. The sculptures relate to the ancient Czech legends and their topics occur also in the works of the foremost Czech composers

One of the best educated composers of the second half of the 19th century was Zdeněk Fibich who lived in Prague. Like Smetana he too supported the idea of programme music and especially the new conception of opera. By his nature, however, he was a sheer romantic who was also close to extreme and hot eroticism. Beside operas The Bride from Messina, Hedy, Šárka, The Fall of Arkun and others by which he enriched the repertoire of the National Theatre, he created a worldwide unique work – a trilogy of a stage melodrama Hippodamia according to ancient topic with lyrics by Jaroslav Vrchlický (1853–1912). Premieres of individual dramas based on transfer of the Wagner-type musical and dramatic principle to the field of melodrama took place in the National Theatre (The Courtship of Pelopos 21 February, 1890, The Reconciliation of Tantalos 2 June, 1891, The Death of Hippodamia 8 November, 1891). Like Jaroslav Vrchlický and Julius Zeyer (1841–1901) who were members of the so-called Lumír generation also Fibich strove for a synthesis of the world and Czech topics trying to extend the field of themes of the Czech art by problems and ideas which are valid in generally human terms.

Due to the works by Smetana, Dvořák, Fibich and the artistic performances of excellent virtuosos, such as the violoncello player Hanuš Wihan (1855–1920) and violinist František Ondříček (1857–1922) to name the artist fully pertaining to the Prague musical life, the Czech music acquired its national features which became obligatory for the conception of "Czechism" and cultural identity of the Czech nation also in the future years. At the same time, it was art which managed to rise above the restricted framework of the national isolation and won the world's recognition.

In the modern period

Near the Main Railway Station in Prague is the Neo-Renaissance building of the State Opera. It was built according to the designs of the Viennese architects Hermann Helmer and Ferdinand Fellner for the purposes of the New German Theatre in Prague. The front bears busts by the sculptor Otto Mentzel and in the gable is a group of carriages – Dionysos and Thalia by Theodor Friedel. The orchestra produced also philharmonic concerts

The interior of the State Opera. The New German Theatre played a significant role in the production of the music by Richard Strauss and Gustav Mahler in Prague. Moreover, their music was accepted also by the Czech musical environment. The orchestra of the theatre was in immediate touch with Mahler which contributed considerably to the creation of Mahler's cult in Prague. German Modernism was produced here in the period between the two world wars and in 1936 this scene produced for the first time outside the Soviet Union Shostakovich's opera Lady Macbeth of Mzensk

Until the first world war the Czech music lived as a national minority surrounded by the expansive German culture struggling hard for its existence within the framework of the Austrian-Hungarian monarchy. Prague played a positive role in this struggle: it became the point of intersection of everything that had crucial influence on the general development of music in Europe. National cultures were already formulated, liberation movements ceased to be its driving force, the influence of church on musical culture discontinued, at long last music could develop by itself from its own inspiration sources and establish contacts with the world. Despite this fact its homogeneity, as compared with previous centuries, was disintegrating, splintering, differentiated in terms of value which was caused by capitalization of a great number of music activities.

In the period of 1905–1912 a representative edifice of the City of Prague called Municipal House (Obecní dům) was under construction in the vicinity of the Powder Gate. Its architects were Antonín Balšánek and Osvald Polívka. The decoration was participated by the foremost Czech artists. From its beginning the house served to the significant social and cultural events of the city. In January 1918, in the Smetana hall, the deputies of the Czech lands declared the so-called Three-Magi Declaration (Tříkrálová deklarace) requiring independence of the state and then on 28 October, 1918 the first laws of the Czechoslovak Republic were declared here. On 30 October, 1918, here was the first performance of the significant symphony "Ripening" by Josef Suk produced by the Czech Philharmonic Orchestra and Václav Talich

Since the beginning of the 20th century in Prague there was a sharp extension of the institutional and operation base which is so important for the development of various music activities. In 1902 the representative building of the Prague Hlahol society was opened. In 1907 operation was started of the City Theatre in Royal Vinohrady which also became an opera stage for twelve years. In 1911 a new representative edifice was built in Art Nouveau style called Municipal House (Obecní dům) with the greatest concert hall in the then Prague – the Smetana Hall. But also in other parts of Prague, especially in the suburbs, new concert and theatre halls were built which made it possible to intensify the musical life of the city. Besides, new publishing

houses and musical pedagogical institutes were founded in Prague. Also the circumstance that from 1901 the director of the Prague conservatoire was Antonín Dvořák increased extraordinarily not only the prestige of this institute but also increased the standard of the musical activities in many fields, particularly in the field of creative work of the composers.

Thanks to the establishment of the Czech Quartet at the Prague conservatoire supported and observed by Antonín Dvořák (the original members were Karel Hoffmann (1872–1936), Josef Suk (1874–1935), Oskar Nedbal (1874–1930) and Otto Berger (1873–1897), soon after Berger's death their hitherto professor of violoncello and

The interior of the Municipal House. The architectonic layout of the Rieger hall was designed by Osvald Polívka and the paintings were produced by Max Švabinský who depicted here "The Czech Spring" – ten giants of the Czech culture, i.e. from the left – Svatopluk Čech, Jan Neruda, Jaroslav Vrchlický, Božena Němcová, Julius Zeyer, Josef Václav Myslbek, Mikoláš Aleš, Josef Mánes, Bedřich Smetana and Antonín Dvořák. The bust of Ladislav Rieger is a work by Josef Václav Myslbek

PRAŽSKÉ JARO

The interior of the Municipal House is a work of the foremost Czech artists of the early 20th century. This is a part of Smetana hall: the wall paintings by Karel Špillar, the sculpture and stucco decoration of the balcony by Karel Novák, the relief (František Škroup, the author of the Czech national anthem) by Josef Kalvoda

chamber play Hanuš Wihan started to co-operate with the quartet and provided it with an exceptional artistic standard) the Czech Society for Chamber Music was founded two years later and immediately developed a rich concert activity. Until the establishment of the Czechoslovak Republic in 1918 it held 208 concerts in Prague which was unprecedented when taking into account the small number of concerts in the previous years. The events of the society were participated by all Czech chamber bodies, foremost soloists and a number of bodies from abroad.

Soon the Czech Quartet developed into a modern body, the first of its kind in this country (later Nedbal as viola player was succeeded by Jiří Herod, 1875–1934, and Wihan was succeeded by

Smetana hall is the centre of the Municipal House. Concerts of the foremost Czech and world musical bodies take place in this hall as well as the productions of the Prague Spring international music festival. The importance of the hall corresponds with its artistic and sculptural decorations by František Ženíšek, Karel Špillar and Ladislav Šaloun

Ladislav Zelenka, 1881–1957) which by its impressive performances promoted the notion of the Czech chamber art in this country as well as abroad. Many other bodies were founded under its influence, such as Ševčík–Lhotský Quartet, Herold Quartet, Ondříček Quartet, The Czech Trio and others. The activity of the Czech Quartet was tremendous. Although thanks to its tours this ensemble ranked among the world's best acknowledged quartets at all it never lost contact with the Prague audience. This was due to its perfect interpretation of the Czech chamber literature – its repertoire base consisted, in particular, of the works by Smetana and Dvořák and later it was extended systematically by other works of the Czech modern music.

Like in the past, in the periods of the Baroque and Classicism, many musicians – usually those

BO
JOV
NOST

The Municipal House – the Mayor hall, the paintings are the work of the foremost Art Nouveau artist Alfons Mucha. The section paintings depict civic virtues represented by the personalities from the Czech history. Here, the Bohemian king George of Poděbrady representing Independence, and the Hussite commander John Roháč of Dubá – Resistance

The Municipal House – The Mayor hall. In view of decoration, the hall is considered to be the most beautiful room in the builidng. The author of its architectonic layout was Osvald Polívka, the painting were made by Alfons Mucha. The mascorons with crowned girl head and the symbol of Prague, the section paintings represent civis cirtues – Battle spirit John Žižka of Trocnov to the left and Faithfulness John Amos Comenius to the right

The architectonic layout of the Grégr hall of the Municipal House designed by Osvald Polívka is supported by the wonderful painting decoration by František Ženíšek. The wall painting shows The War Song from the triptych called The Love, War and Funeral Songs

poor but talented – left Prague for the world, also in this new era many artists left Prague to get recognition on the world arenas. However, there was a substantial difference between the former and the latter phenomena. While in the past the Czech musicians went abroad in great numbers due to social necessity or due to religious persecution now they left Prague mainly because they wanted to get appraisal of the big world of educated people and to try the taste of world fame since as artists they belonged to the world's top. The most distinctive and indeed supranational personalities included, for instance, the quite exceptional singers, the tenor Karel Burian (1870–1924), sopranos Berta Foerstrová-Lautererová (1869–1936) and Emma Destinn (1878–1930), the violinist with brilliant technique Jan Kubelík (1880–1940) and his more lyrical colleague Jaroslav Kocian (1883–1950) and many others. Without denying their origin and the Czech roots of their mastery they returned to the Czech metropolis as if they were connected with it by an invisible, inspiring umbilical cord. From the 1890s until the outbreak of the world war fire Prague was visited also by numerous foreign artists, such as the pianists Tereza Careňo, Alfred Grünfeld (1852–1924), Eugen d Albert (1864–1932), the conductor stars V. I. Safonov (1852–1918), Hans Richter (1843–1916), Arthur Nikisch (1855–1922) as well as great composer personalities, such as Eduard Grieg (1843–1907), Richard Strauss (1864–1949), Gustav Mahler

The front of the buildings from the early 20th century at Masaryk embankment. The house with the remarkable Art Nouveau gable belongs to the most genuine Art Nouveau architectonic monuments. The edifice of the Prague Hlahol society was finished in 1905 according to a project by the architect Josef Fanta. Mostly it was built from money raised in favour of the Hlahol society and gifts of its supporters. Beside the mosaic at the front gable the house is decorated also by a mosaic above the entrance

The interior in the house of the Prague Hlahol society at Masaryk embankment. The hall is dominated by a painting from 1921 by the artist Alfons Mucha called Song with an inscription above it "For the purpose of choir rehearsals built by Hlahol in 1905 A.D. in the 45th year of its activity" and the motto of this significant musical society "Through singing to the heart, through the heart to the homeland"

The facade of the Prague Hlahol building is decorated also by statues of the sculptor Josef Pekárek and by ornaments by Karel Mottl. From its establishment in 1861 Hlahol was supported by the foremost personalities of the Czech social life and culture. Significant musicians worked in it and under their influence the society became an excellent choral ensemble – the best renowned choir-leaders include Karel Bendl, Karel Knittl and Bedřich Smetana. Even today numerous social events and regular concerts take part in the rooms of the Hlahol building

Vinohradské Theatre in the district of Vinohrady. The edifice of the theatre was built in 1904–1907. The author of the project Alois Čenský focused in his design on the contemporary Art Nouveau liking. A big hood with supports in the form of spirals richly decorated with plant Art Nouveau decoration and with pendants is projecting from the huge front into the square (náměstí Míru) over the entrance. The front of the building has its crown in a couple of pylons with symbolical groups. A great variety of significant personalities of the Czech artistic life were active in the theatre

(1860–1911), Ferrucio Busoni (1866–1924) and Arnold Schönberg (1874–1951). Prague accepted their works with apprehension, with understanding of a really advanced audience as was typical of it already from the time of Mozart.

From 1900 when Karel Kovařovic (1862–1920) became the chief of opera of the National Theatre there was a radical change of the repertoire management and of the interpretation face of this highly prestige opera ensemble. Kovařovic required from all musical bodies and opera soloists a perfect professionalism and artistic discipline, he managed to rehabilitate a number of less frequently played operas (Smetana's Dalibor and The Devil's Wall, Dvořák's Dimitrij and Fibich's The Bride from Messina), he presented many new operas including Dvořák's The Water Nymph, Ostrčil's operas The Death of Vlasta and The Eyes of Kunál, Foerster's Jessika, Novák's Karlštejn and many others. He was a demanding and extraordinarily dramatic conductor, his interpretation creations were rich in almost romantic soundness and exceptional colourfulness. When in 1901 the National Theatre orchestra went on strike due to their social situation he dismissed it even though its social requirements were not unjustified. Then these abruptly unemployed musicians established the Czech Philharmonic

The memorial of Vítězslav Novák in the Petřín orchard is a work by Josef Gočár. Vítězslav Novák (1870–1949) belonged to the representatives of the Czech modern music. The advantage of this Modernism is that it managed to cope with the national tradition and the folk music culture. The main representatives Leoš Janáček, Josef Bohuslav Foerster, Otakar Ostrčil, Josef Suk and Vítězslav Novák managed to assimilate also the initiatives of the top musical trends of the European musical development. Thanks to his inspiration by the Moravian and Slovak folk songs, Vítězslav Novák arrived at a synthesis of the Czech Modernism at a high professional standard

Orchestra as a body with a stable membership of professional players. The Czech Philharmonic Orchestra controlled jointly by Ludvík V. Čelanský (1870–1931) and Oskar Nedbal (1874–1930) but chiefly by Dr. Vilém Zemánek (1875–1922) played an important role in the pre-war and wartime musical life even though – to be true – due to the continuous struggle for mere survival its artistic standard was not the highest. Despite this fact it fulfilled what was expected of it: as the only one independent symphonic body in this country it made the Prague audience familiar with the widest repertoire of the Czech and world music. At the same time, it provoked to life a number of new symphonic and orchestral compositions without which today we cannot imagine the development of the Czech modern music.

The wonderful and unique atmosphere of the Baroque Kaiserstein palace seems to be urging organizing of concerts and performances, such as this gala production. Prominent singers, ballet and chamber ensemble – all of them in period costumes – of the Original Musical Theatre Prague

It cannot be omitted that from certain time also the musical life of the German minority started to gain independence. In 1888 the Prague Germans built in the very centre of the city their New German Theatre (Neues Deutsches Theater, today the State Opera) whose orchestra organized also philharmonic concerts. Upon the model of the Czech Society for Chamber Music they also established the German Society for Chamber Music. They were engaged in building of their own music school system and as amateurs they worked in sing societies which, unfortunately, from time to time turned into centres of the German national chauvinism. Although this base for the production of German music in Prague

After the year 1700 the architect Giovanni Battista Alliprandi built a palace in the lower part of Lesser Quarter square. The attic bears statues of the four seasons. The palace is famous for the fact that the Czech singer Emma Destinn lived here. Her bust by Jan Simota is placed on the front facade. Here the famous singer came back from her journeys for fame – from the New York Metropolitan Opera where her artistic partner on stage was the famous singer Enrico Caruso, from the Berlin Hofoper or the Paris Opera theatres

was rather strong and economically ensured it did not produce any big musical personality. If some real personalities appeared within the framework of the musical activities of the German minority they were mostly imported to Prague from the neighbouring Germany or Austria-Hungary. This was also the case of popularity in Prague of the music of Richard Strauss and Gustav Mahler whose works were later accepted also by the Czech musical environment. Extraordinary events of world significance were, in particular, the production of Strauss's operas Salome and Electra in 1906 and 1910 in the Prague National Theatre, then in 1907 the Czech Philharmonic Orchestra presented Mahler's Symphony No. 4 and, a year later, on 19 September, 1908 also the world pre-

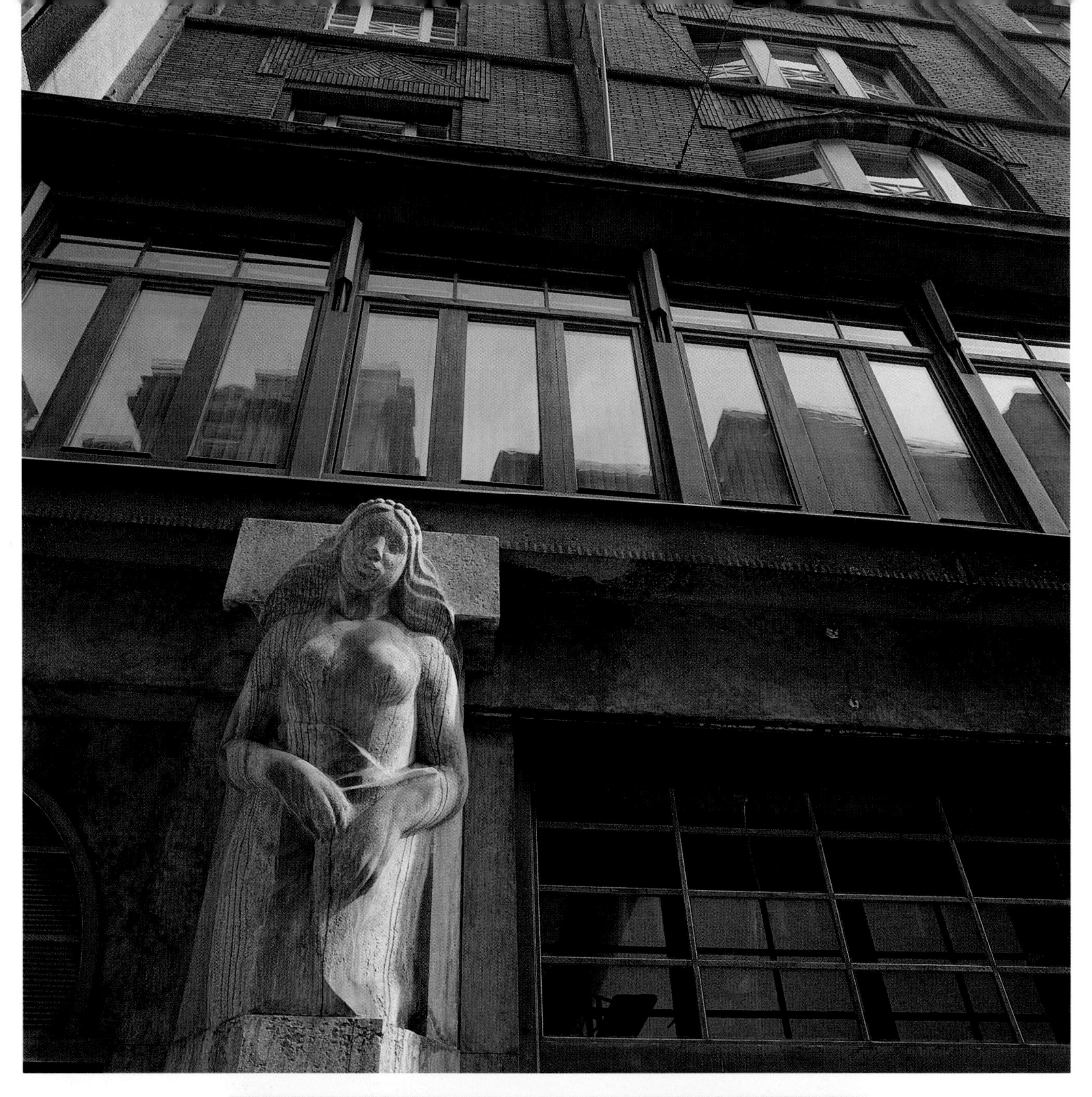

Also this house No. 748/30 in Jungmannova Street called Mozarteum has its importance in the Czech history of music. The construction of the building was ordered by Mojmír Urbánek in 1911–1913 for the needs of his musical publishing house with a concert hall. The building designed by the architect Jan Kotěra is a piece of architectonic Modernism in Prague. The ground floor of the building is decorated with a couple of woman sculptures by Jan Štursa

Musical motifs can be found in Prague also on the facades of the suburban tenement houses. This house in the Prague district of Michle has an entrance lined with big stucco statues of musicians with guitar and mandolin. It was built in 1913 by the builder Ludvík Melzer. It is a Late-Art Nouveau construction with already Cubist rhombic elements on the facade and in the decoration of the interior of the house

miere of the Symphony No. 7 conducted by the author. But mainly, the orchestra of the New German Theatre with conductors L. Blech (1870–1958) and O. Klemperer (1885–1973) maintained immediate contacts with Mahler, hence contributing substantially to the formation of Mahler's cult in Prague.

The advent of the New Modernism in music in the period from the end of the last century until World War One was something that elevated highly the musical standard of Prague and made it also in the creative field a place of spiritual interests and clashes comparable with the creative streams elsewhere in Europe. The merit of this Czech Modernism was that it managed to cope with the national tradition and the folk music culture, that it did not stagnate on eclecticism and conservatism dictated by extreme sticking to the continuation of the composer orientations in the spirit of Bedřich Smetana and Antonín Dvořák. The main representatives of this Czech modern music – Josef Bohuslav Foerster (1859–1951), Vítězslav Novák (1870–1949), Josef Suk (1874–1935), Otakar Ostrčil (1879–1935) and in Moravia Leoš Janáček (1854–1928) – managed, in particular, to assimilate the impulses of the top trends of the European musical development from the circle of production of Richard Strauss, Gustav Mahler and Claude Debussy (1862–1918). This was even in a time when the Czech public and its politicians struggled hard to defend the national existence against the German-Austrian pressures. Not all of these authors lived for the whole time in Prague but this was not important. Although in 1893–1919 Josef Bohuslav Foerster worked abroad close to Gustav Mahler in Hamburg and in Vienna he influenced the Czech musical character by his noble music and richness of his melodies (especially, his choir works got popular). Leoš Janáček, one of most original personalities of the then Czech music did not manage to assert himself in Prague until 1916 (due to twelve-years long Kovařovic's dislike to perform Janáček's opera Her Step-Daughter (Její pastorkyňa) on the stage of the Prague National Theatre). His music is comparable with any authors within the world context. Vítězslav Novák went through both the influence of the musical Impressionism and the influence of the works by Richard Strauss but thanks to his inspiration by the Moravian and Slovak folk songs he later arrived at a synthesis of the Czech modern development at a high professional standard by which as an excellent pedagogue at the Prague conservatoire he influenced a whole generation of younger composers. Josef Suk, initially the most melodious and most accessible of all his contemporaries, created a new type of the Czech modern symphony. Otakar Ostrčil, by his emotional unpretentiousness and deeply thought constructivism was closest to the production of the second Vienna school of Schönberg and Berger type but he did not conform with it. These Czech authors, by their richly branched production from songs, choirs up to symphonies, cantatas and operas gave an original character to the Czech modern music not only by their creative coping with the European contemporary artistic trends but also by the fact that they managed to maintain that amazing development and creative concentration of the Czech music as such.

The Art Nouveau and Cubist house in the Prague district of Nusle, Boleslavova Street No. 9 by the Prague architect Karel Hannauer from 1913–1914. The rhombic and finger-fish decoration on the facade is supplemented with Late-Art Nouveau plastic decoration of the front gable and tiny children figures with musical instruments at the level of the first floor

ANTIQUES
galerie

After the year 1918

The house No. 48 in Mostecká Street bears a bust of the concert master Ladislav Zelenka. In 1913–1932 this Czech violoncellist was a member of the world known Czech Quartet. As a soloist he ranked among the brilliant interpreters of Dvořák's violoncello concert. He was also the professor of chamber play and violoncello play at the master school of the Prague conservatoire (later Academy of Performing Arts)

The establishment of the Czechoslovak Republic on 28 October, 1918 brought also many changes to the musical situation in Prague. The Czech capital belonged no more to the multinational confederation of states with hegemony of Germanism. All its cultural life could focus freely on the development of those musical activities in which the newly born republic was immediately interested. Prague, the capital of all the particular lands including Bohemia, Moravia, Silesia, Slovakia and the Sub-Carpathian Ukraine remained the natural centre of the most important and best representative musical activities. Through the Ministry of Schools and National Education the musical matters were controlled centrally. The Prague conservatoire was nationalized as well as the National Theatre ten years later. Beside the confiscation of the Estates Theatre for the needs of the Czech drama and opera, further musical institutions were established throughout Prague, such as the Society for Modern Music (1920), Association for Contemporary Music "Přítomnost" (1924), the Czech section of the International Society for Contemporary Music (1922), the Czech Music Society, etc. Also, museums of significant musical personalities connected with Prague were established gradually, such as the Bedřich Smetana Museum, Antonín Dvořák Museum, Mozart's Community in Czechoslovakia with residence in the Bertramka villa, etc.

Just like the Kovařovic era in the National Theatre in 1901–1919, after the establishment of Czechoslovakia there was a new era also in this most significant domestic institution. Otakar Ostrčil was elected the chief of opera. He was at its head continuously until April 1935. However, the nervous situation did not leave him in peace for this work. On the one hand, Ostrčil presented consistently the Czech classical and modern musical dramatic works (cycles of Smetana's and Dvořák's operas, premieres of Janáček's, Foerster's, Novák's and his own works, e. g. John's Kingdoms) but he had to struggle with political reaction which tried to boycott the Expressionistic production of the type of Berg's Vojcek.

After Ostrčil's death in 1935, the hitherto chief of the Czech Philharmonic Orchestra Václav Talich (1883–1961) became the chief of the opera of the National Theatre. The era of his management is connected with the hardest period of the National Theatre when he had to struggle not only against the increasing opposition against his person from the domestic opponents (e. g. Zdeněk Nejedlý, Mirko Očadlík and others) but under the Nazi occupation also from the Czech fascists (e. g. the so-called Flag-bearers) and the pro-Nazi, collaborating minister Emanuel Moravec. Talich's repertoire management was being curtailed, each word being censored, some works were withdrawn from the repertoire upon order of the higher political authorities (Libuše, The Brandenburgers in Bohemia, Dimitrij, The Dog-Heads, Fidelio, etc.). Although Talich worked in the hardest time he stuck with fanatic faith to artistic perfection of all the performances as if it was this in which consisted the resistance strength of culture in this politically restless and for the Czech nation tragic time. His staging of Dvořák's The Water Nymph, Martinů's Julietta, Janáček's Katya Kabanova and The Cunning Little Vixen, Smetana's Libuše (as long as it was allowed to be played), The Bartered Bride, The Secret, Dvořák's Jakobin, Beethoven's Fidelio (before it was prohibited by censors) as well as Mozart's operas were the supreme artistic creations which had remained unsurpassed in the theatre for a long time. An extraordinarily artistic and political-resistance event was the organizing of the musical May in 1939 and in the following years by which Talich in the connection of the bodies of the National Theatre and the Czech Philharmonic Orchestra demonstrated how it is necessary to work in the time of political non-freedom. These festivals held exclusively under Talich's control with manifestation response and prohibited from 1943 by the occupation authorities contributed by their idea to the establishment of the international festival Prague Spring in the post-war, free situation. Under Talich's management of the National Theatre opera a generation of excellent singers was brought up here most of which became bearers of a high artistic standard of the representative Czech opera also in the first post-war years. We can mention, for instance, Beno Blachut (born 1913), Jaroslav Gleich (born 1900), Eduard Haken (born 1910), Ota Horáková (born 1904), Karel Kalaš (born 1910), Marta Krásová (born 1901), Zdeněk Otava (born 1902), Marie Podvalová (born 1909), Theodor Šrubař (born 1917), Marie Tauberová (born 1911) and others. As professor of conducting in the master school of the Prague conservatoire (from 1932) Talich brought up also a whole generation of superb domestic and foreign conductors who later became the pride of many symphonic orchestras or opera houses.

An important supplement of the musical life in the years between the two wars was also the continuing activity of the New German Theatre. This institute enriched the Prague musical life particularly with its re-

This Neo-Renaissance building constructed originally according to a project of Antonín Wiehl for the Prague waterworks is in a close vicinity of the Old Town mills above the river. Since 1936 it is Smetana Museum and, at the same time, it is the centre of research and documentation of the work of Bedřich Smetana. The entrance to the museum is from the Street Novotného lávka which provides also perhaps the most beautiful view of the typical Prague panorama

OPERA MOZART
THEATRE & TICKETS
KLUB LÁVKA

Turandot is the last opera by the world-renowned author and the leading representative of the so-called Verism Giacomo Puccini. The author selected a fairy tale topic for its composition about a Chinese princess Turandot applying a wide range of poetic, picturesque, exotic, grotesque and passionate motives. The premiere of the work took place on 24th April, 1926 in Milan and shortly after this it was played also in the Prague National Theatre. This performance is from the present-day State Opera in Prague. In the closing scene the story achieves a catharsis when Turandot puts an end to the power of cruelty in China introducing the power of love

pertoire management. It was chiefly thanks to the Austrian composer and conductor Alexander Zemlinsky (1872–1942) who headed the opera ensemble for sixteen years (1911–1927) that this theatre produced the German Modernism so that Prague had the opportunity to hear in time the works by Ernst Křenek (born 1900), Arnold Schönberg (1874–1951) (on 6 June, 1924 the author's monodrama Awaiting had its world premiere here), Paul Hindemith (1895–1963) as composer and conductor of his own works. This theatre performed for the first time outside the Soviet Union Shostakovich's opera Lady Macbeth of Mzensk after the novel by N. Leskov which was denounced shortly after.

Among the Czech artists Václav Talich was a conductor who in the modern time influenced most of all the original profile of the Czech musical reproduction as such. His work as conductor and repertoire manager with the Czech Philharmonic Orchestra (from 1919 to 1941 with the exception of two seasons he was its artistic chief) played the most distinct role in the artistic maturing of the Czech musical interpretation art. Talich was thoroughly familiar with the pedagogical and analytical principles of Otakar Ševčík (he was a leaver of his violin class), was a friend of and expert in the Czech Quartet (from time to time he worked with the quartet as the second violinist) and had experience as concert master in the philharmonic orchestra of Arthur Nikisch (1855–1922). Due to all these qualities Talich developed the Czech Philharmonic Orchestra into a top ensemble of a world standard which was appraised also abroad during its tours to foreign countries or during the Prague festivals of the International Society for Contemporary Music in which this body was significantly engaged. However, for the development of the Czech reproduction art in the symphonic field it was also important that the Czech repertoire (particularly Smetana, Dvořák, Suk, Novák, Janáček, Foerster, Ostrčil) was performed in model interpretation. Thanks to the Czech Philharmonic Orchestra headed by Václav Talich and from 1935 also in co-operation with Rafael Kubelík (born 1914) Prague could already from the beginning of the new cultural life in the free republic count on regular orchestral concerts which formed the backbone of every concert season. This was enabled also thanks to the fact that its economic situation which had been so hard in the past was at least partly settled in the new time because it received regular subsidies from the state and the city and from 1927 it ensured regular co-operation with the Czechoslovak Radio.

Soon after World War One Prague got familiar also with the top works of both the German and French Modernism – the authors of the so-called Paris Six – and with the music by Igor Stravinski (1882–1971) and Sergei Sergeievitch Prokofiev (1891–1953). After the Prague premiere of Petrushka in the National Theatre in 1925 Stravinski visited Prague several times on the occasion of the concerts of his works. Similarly,

Prokofiev's art influenced strongly the vanguard atmosphere of the Prague musical environment. In 1924 his First Violin Concerto was performed here, in January 1932 the author performed here his Piano Concerto No. 3 and in 1936 his Piano Concerto No. 1. Study of the music of these authors influenced, in particular, Bohuslav Martinů (1890–1959) who after his initial work in Prague (among others in the Czech Philharmonic Orchestra under Talich) moved to Paris. The war and the curious political situation after 1948 caused that although he became a world-renowned author he had never come back home again.

Beside the authors of the older generation (Foerster, Suk, Novák, Ostrčil and in Moravia Janáček) who as mature personalities maintained the continuity of the top Czech music, it was particularly

The tenement house No. 152 in Francouzská Street in the Prague district of Vinohrady was the place of living of the brilliant Czech conductor of the Czech Philharmonic Orchestra Václav Talich. This significant Czech artist was, in particular, an artist who in the modern times influenced most of all the original profile of the Czech musical production as such

Alois Hába (1893–1973) who in the era between the wars managed to create a counterpart to the second Vienna school, thus focusing the attention of the European Modernism on Prague. His "athematic" style excluding the principle of repetition of themes, his harmony with tonal centres but, in particular, the creation of several systems of micro-interval manner of creation (quarter tone, sixth tone, twelfth tone, etc.) whose practical use inspired Hába to a construction of new musical instruments – led him also to the opening of an independent class of quarter tone music at the Prague conservatoire. This became famous in no time attracting many domestic as well as foreign young composers. Hába based his theory of micro-interval creation on a thorough study of the folklore of the eastern and oriental nations. He tried to promote the justi-

fication of his conviction mainly by his work. One of his most interesting works was his quarter tone opera The Mother based on a raw village theme the premiere of which in 1932 in Munich became one of the biggest cultural events of the European Modernism at all.

Like the Prague violin school of Otakar Ševčík which achieved world renown in the period between the two world wars, also the piano school of Vilém Kurz (1872–1945) reached world fame. His pupils in the Prague conservatoire included both the phenomenal performer of modern piano literature Ervín Schulhoff (1894–1942) and Rudolf Firkušný (1912–1994) who as the first of the Czech pianists managed to get among the world top and also as Janáček's pupil he became an authentic bearer of the reproduction conception of the piano works of this master. But also the pianist Jan Heřman (1866–1946), the violinist Váša Příhoda (1900–1937) and the National Theatre bass singer Vilém Zítek (1890–1956) belonged to the category of exceptional, worldwide acknowledged personalities.

Jaroslav Ježek (1906–1942), the musical composer, brilliant piano player and co-creator of Osvobozené Theatre of Jiří Voskovec and Jan Werich lived in Kaprova Street No. 10/45. His satirical and political songs are a world unique phenomenon in its dancing and jazz genre. The so-called blue room has been preserved in this house where the almost blind composer created his works

However, with the coming closer of World War Two and with the still stronger and stronger endangering of the European states by Hitler's Germany, Prague was still more and more becoming a centre of the worldwide acknowledged but persecuted artists. Until the last while, 15 March, 1939 before its occupation by the Nazi Wehrmacht it was the only place in the neighbourhood of the fascist Germany where democratic relations were still preserved. Many of the artists concentrated here fled in time before fascism, others died as a result of the ruthless racist persecutions during the Nazi occupation.

The occupied Prague, the suffering Prague, Prague which was to be Germanized defended itself during the Nazi occupation. This was done not only by honouring and performing all cultural values reminding the home, homeland, national tradition, freedom, resistance but also by a new creative production which was set into a self-preserving function to defend the nation. It was democratised. The Czech composers threw away anything that was too difficult and too artistic, they worked with quotations, known motifs, used various allusions, charades and puzzles as extra-musical symbols where all of this was a certain type of protest against the existing situation. In this hard time the Czech authors living in Prague created two types of musical works: the first one was designed for the current moment with the intention to encourage the audience which was humiliated everyday by the Nazi despotism while the other was to be an artistic document for the future. These outstanding works from the occupation period included, for instance, Novák's compositions De profundis for orchestra, St. Wenceslas triptych for organ and orchestra, the May Symphony, Karel's Revolutionary Overture, Foerster's Cantata 1945, Kabeláč's cantata No Retreat!, Doubrava's Stalingrad Symphony and the seditious piano sonata No. 2, Reiner's piano sonata No. 2 Victory, Jeremiáš's cantata Song for Native Country, Hanuš's opera Flames and many others. The most admirable thing was that the Czech authors were able to compose even in the time between the Gestapo interrogations – for instance using charcoal and toilet paper when other writing instruments were not available. In this way Rudolf Karel (1885–1945) outlined in the Prague Pankrác prison a whole opera The Three Hair of the Old Man Know-All based on the fairy-tale topic by K. J. Erben and created here also his Nonet with dedication to the Czech nonet. He died under tragic circumstances in the Small Fortress of the Terezín concentration camp.

Many authors and concert artists who lived in Prague until the Nazi occupation did not live to see liberation. Some of them died due to their resistance movement activity, others as a result of the so-called Nuremberg race laws. These included the above-mentioned Prague composers Rudolf Karel and Ervín Schulhoff and composers persecuted for their race Viktor Ullmann (1898–1944), Gideon Klein (1919–1944), Hans Krása (1899–1944) and the talented musicologist and viola player Zdeněk Němec (1914–1945) tortured to death by the Nazis for his newspaper treatise about the prophetic mission of Smetana's My Country after one of the concerts of the Czech Philharmonic Orchestra. In emigration in the United States, one of the greatest losses was Jaroslav Ježek (1906–1942), a colleague of the actors and playwrights Voskovec and Werich in the pre-war

Liberated Theatre (Osvobozené divadlo) in Prague. This exceptionally inventive author composed for them dozens of satirical and political songs which got popular in no time and which – even though prohibited by the censors – belonged to the most popular song repertoire of the Czech people (even in the concentration camps!). The composer Vít Nejedlý (1912–1945), author of an extraordinarily good opera The Websters died on the Soviet front in the fight for the Dukla pass at the Czechoslovak border. From among the song composers, Karel Hašler (1879–1941) was tortured to death in the Mauthausen concentration camp under terrible circumstances. He was a singer and actor in the Prague popular cabarets and in the time of non-freedom his song "That Czech Song of Ours" ("Ta naše písnička česká") often fulfilled the function of the Czech unofficial national anthem. All these were immense losses for the Czech culture and the musical life of Prague.

With a certain time distance it appears that the Czech-German musical life of Prague which in a certain symbiosis and with occasional tension lasted for centuries was not cancelled only in 1945 after the resettlement of the Germans from the liberated Czechoslovak Republic but even sooner. In fact, the cancellation of the German musical culture in Prague was a work of the German National Socialists themselves. In their extreme chauvinism they did not admit that the bonds between the Czech and the German musicians would bring fruit on the basis of equal and trustworthy partnership co-operation. They had quite different intentions for the case that they would win

the war. Prague should be a city with prevailing German population, a city which by its beauty and wonderful monuments of architecture untouched by war would serve only to the representatives of the Third Empire. Despite this fact, after 15 March, 1939 almost all significant musicians representing up to that time the German music and co-operating in a creative manner with the Czech environment were resettled, they were driven out from the public and artistic life, drawn to concentration camps, prisons or detention camps. The natural centre of the Prague German life in the New German Theatre was disintegrated, the German magazine Auftakt ceased to be published and its editor-in-chief Erich Steinhard (1886–1941) died in the gas chamber in Chelm, the German academy of music and visual arts in Prague was suddenly useless

and without real artistic personalities. Beside Steinhard who lectured on music history, another of the significant pedagogues in this German high school Konrad Wallerstein (1879–1944), teacher of opera singing, died in the Auschwitz concentration camp. Many of the performance musicians and singers of German nationality living in Prague were not allowed even in this time of German expansion to continue to develop fruitful contacts between the Czech and German cultures on the former basis. Also, everything new, progressive, vanguard, from jazz to compositions in the spirit of the European Modernism of the 20s and 30s was declared by the Nazis as "entartete Kunst" – undesired art. This surprising and seemingly illogical fact, however, requires careful and thorough study so that it would be possible to make an objective evaluation of it.

The Vltava embankment is dominated by the edifice of the National Theatre which at all times remained a natural tabernacle of culture and music. In its vicinity, on the groud floor of the Lažanský palace, is the famous theatre coffee-house Slavie, a place of meetings of artists, and nearby also is the Mánes builidng in the Constructivism style which was built by the artistic society for its own purposes. We cannot fail to mention the Žofín palace at the Slavonic Isle with its tradition of Czech balls and concerts

The view from the Letná plain of a part of Dvořákovo and Alšovo embankments. This area is dominated by the noble edifice of the Rudolphinum which is open with its side front to Prague Castle. In the place of the magnificent embankment there used to be the periphery of the medieval Old and Jewish Towns called Na Rejdišti as evidenced by the name of the street

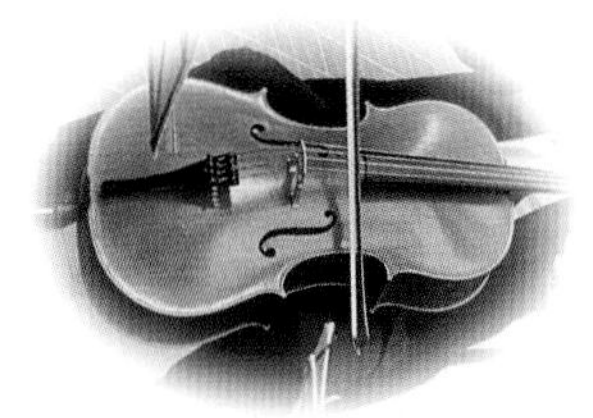

After the year 1945

The first years after the liberating war bring unexpected euphoria also to the musical life in Prague. The Czech Philharmonic Orchestra becomes the state orchestra and moves its residence to the former parliament building – the Rudolphinum (Rafael Kubelík remains to be its artistic chief). Also, the Symphonic Orchestra of the Capital City of Prague FOK headed by the conductor Dr. Václav Smetáček (born 1906) starts to develop. The Great 5th May Opera starts to create vanguard performances in the building of the former New German Theatre. Václav Talich (after a "purgati-

The vast Liechtenstein palace occupies the whole rear part of Malostranské square. Today it is theresidence of the musical department of the Academy of Performing Arts and chamber and orchestral concerts of the students are held here also for the general public

The architect Josef Schulz is the author of the project of Dvořák music hall in the Prague Rudolphinum. Its tall column surrounding is derived from the interior of the Versailles chateau theatre. It is considered to be the finest Prague interior of the 19th century. Since 1945 Dvořák hall has been the residence of the Czech Philharmonic Orchestra which was brought to the world standard by its conductors – Václav Talich, Rafael Kubelík, Karel Ančerl or Václav Neumann. Here we can see a concert of the Czech Philharmonic Orchestra

ve" lawsuit when he was accused by the Communists of collaboration with the Nazis) brings new impulses not only to the opera of the National Theatre (particularly his production of Janáček's Katya Kabanova was impressive) but by his newly established Czech Chamber Orchestra whose members were the new leavers of the Prague conservatoire he established a high artistic standard as a model for all future chamber orchestras in the environment of a fast developing Prague musical life. The first years of the international festival Prague Spring whose artistic guarantor became the Czech Philharmonic Orchestra bring rapidly to Prague dozens of superb musical artists,

The originally Gothic church of St. Simon and Judas near the Brethren of Mercy monastery and hospital, which was adapted later in the Baroque style is frequently visited by the lovers of classic music because today it serves as a concert hall. Here, the members of the famous Pavel Šmok ballet ensemble dance on Stabat mater by Antonín Dvořák

Adjacent to the church of Our Lady Below Chain in the Lesser Quarter is the Grand Priory palace which is the residence of the Grand Prior of the order of the Knights of St. John. The single-storey building was constructed according to the project of the architect Bartolomeo Scotti in 1726–1728. Inside the building is a richly decorated Knight hall which serves also for festive events with music and singing – here the choir of the Church Family and Medical Secondary School of the Blessed Zdislava in Prague

virtuosos and conductors, later also foreign orchestras. The initial most precious moment in the festival was the inspiring meeting of the musical culture of the West and the East. Prague was visited also by excellent artists from the Soviet Union, such as J. Mravinski, I. Oistrach, L. Oborin, E. Gilels and many others. Prague saw a musical revival which was favourably reflected in the richness of its concert and musical theatre life as well as in the establishment of a number of chamber orchestras (such as the later world-renown Smetana, Vlach and other quartets). After the long years of isolation in the period of World War Two, there are also new impulses for the musical authors who are

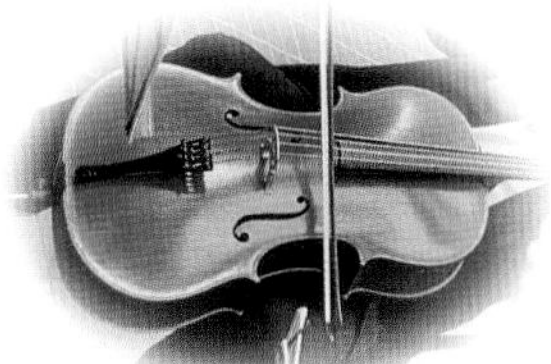

A Baroque match of the Gothic church of Our Lady before Týn in Staroměstské square is the church of St. Nicholas from the end of the first third of the 18th century. The construction was projected by Kilian Ignaz Dienzenhofer and its sculptural decoration was provided by Antonín Braun, the nephew of the famous Matthias Bernard Braun. An interesting fact is that a military concert hall was in this place in the 1860s. Here we can see a performance of the English Portsmouth Grammar School choir in this precious copula construction

The Art Nouveau building at the Prague Exhibition Area, the so-called Pavilion of the Capital City of Prague serves as lapidary of the National Museum. A collection of stone sculptural and architectonic monuments from the 11th to the 19th centuries is placed here. Also this room is used as a concert hall – here the singer Ann K. accompanied by guitars

The National Technological Museum at the Letná plain built in 1938–1941 contains precious collections of machines and technical equipment. This unusual space served as a concert hall for the famous Stamic Quartet in its programme about Antonín Dvořák. By the location of the concert to the museum the organizers wanted to remind the generally known admiration of Dvořák to the civilization progress, locomotives and steamships

coping gradually with the world artistic streams as well as with the works of the excellent representatives of the East and the West who were not played for a long time – for instance with the works by Sergei S. Prokofiev (1891–1953), Dmitri Shostakovich (1906–1975), Béla Bartók (1881–1945), Igor Stravinski (1882–1971), Arthur Honeger (1892–1955), Aron Copland (born 1900), Darius Milhaud (born 1892) and others.

However, this time which was so promising and favourable for the development of musical culture in Prague did not last long. After the coming of the Communists to power in February 1948 the whole field of the Czech

The library hall in the former Old Town convent of the Servites order in St. Michael's church in Melantrichova Street No. 971 can pride itself on the wonderful ceiling fresco from the second half of the 18th century by Josef Hager. At present it is the residence of the schools Týnská škola and Rečkova kolej which organize here concerts of old music – here the musicians from the ensemble Archi di Praga

culture was again under the spell of political declarations about art from which the most notorious and adverse became the so–called Ždanov theses. The production of many composers was declared formalistic and non-democratic (Bohuslav Martinů, Alois Hába, Miloslav Kabeláč (1908–1979), Jaroslav Doubrava (1909–1960), Klement Slavonický (born 1910) and many others), numerous artists left for emigration again (Rafael Kubelík, Rudolf Firkušný, František Smetana (born

1914), Karel Boleslav Jirák (1891–1972), Karel Husa (born 1921), shortly before his death also Karel Ančerl (1908–1979) and others). Václav Talich is prohibited to work in Prague and his so promising Czech Chamber Orchestra is dissolved. The 5th May Opera devoted to vanguard staging (among other also Hába's quarter tone opera The Mother) is merged under a new name Smetana Theatre with the National Theatre. The activities of any societies are prohibited. Traditional musical institutions, such as Přítomnost, Umělecká beseda, Mánes and others associating composers of a certain opinion orientation are liquidated or cannot perform their own concert activities.

Rothmayer hall in Prague Castle is decorated with a statue of T.G. Masaryk (the first Czechoslovak president) by Jan Štursa from 1921 made from white marble. This concert is performed by the world-famous harp player, winner of many international competitions and the Prague conservatoire professor Jana Boušková, pupil of professor Libuše Váchalová

Composers and gradually also musicologists and concert artists are organized in the only one permissible Union of Czechoslovak Composers which is controlled ideologically by the almighty Communist party and whose mission is to implement its policy. After the oppressive and fruitless 50s when public stages were accessible only to the production of the so-called Socialist Realism, it is only in the course of the 60s that there is a release and a new bloom of musical production created as

Regular exchange of guards at the Prague Castle courtyard in front of Matthias Gate. This ceremony is accompanied by the music of the Castle Guard in red uniforms. The Castle Guard music assists also in the invitation ceremonies on the occasion of significant visits of Prague Castle which is the residence of the president of the Czech Republic

D. MATTHIAS EL
ROM. IMP. S. AVG.
HVNG. BOH. REX. &C.
F.F. ANO. MDCXIV

if in the shadow and out of spite in relation to the official requirements of the political authorities. This trend is short but unusually fruitful. However, it was stopped by the occupation of Czechoslovakia by the Soviet troops in August 1968 which meant the liquidation of the so-called Prague spring. This development was coarsely disturbed also by the alleged "normalization" from the part of the totalitarian political regime which deadened almost everything which was vital, hopeful, vanguard and progressive. The artistic average dominated again in all the spheres of musical life. People without the needed moral and top artistic credit took the lead in the artistic institutions. Many artists, particularly their production, were excluded from the active artistic and concert operation. Those years were a period of decay when the progressive, unconventional and artistically valuable works could be created only in the intimacy of households without opportunity to get in touch with a wider musical public.

The political revolution of November 1989 changes all of a sudden the whole structure of the musical life particularly in Prague. Instead of one or two artistic agencies, a whole network of concert consulting management was created. Instead of the only one state gramophone record company dozens of new ones are founded. One concert follows another

Most of the significant Czech composers and musicians lay here side by side at the Vyšehrad cemetery. The so-called Wiehl arcades contain the bust of the most celebrated creator of the Czech music Antonín Dvořák, and the tombstones of the significant singers of the National Theatre from the era of Václav Talich and later periods – Beno Blachut and Eduard Haken

providing unique musical experiences to the mass inflow of foreigners who try to get acquainted with the beauties of Prague and especially its monuments of architecture. The National Theatre which until the revolution included also the Tyl and Smetana Theatres is separated again as the representative stage for the field of opera and drama and the Tyl Theatre is turned again into the Estates Theatre and the Smetana Theatre is turned into the State Opera in Prague. The international festival Prague Spring is gaining new face, too. Czech artists, such as the conductor Rafael Kubelík, the pianist Rudolf Firkušný and the composer Karel Husa come back to their homeland being welcomed as the symbols of free life deprived of the Communist dictatorship. All of a sudden it is a different Prague than that of the past forty years of the totalitarian oppression. It is Prague which is forming again its true spiritual face open to all impulses coming from the inside of its own democratic tradition or from abroad. Prague is ringing with music, sacred and secular, popular and classical. Values are being crystallized and refined. Musical culture is increasing its intensity as never before which is the most marvellous and most optimistic prerequisite of its future musical development within the framework of the democratic society.

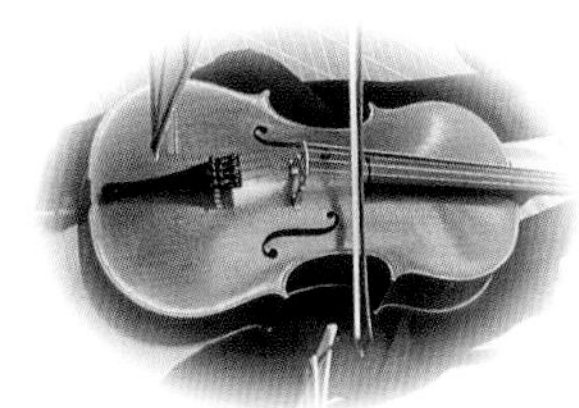

An evening vista from the Slavonic isle (Slovanský ostrov) in the Vltava River. Charming illumination of the National Theatre, a part of the Neo-Baroque and Art Nouveau Legion Bridge and, in the rear, the corner of the Neo-Renaissance Lažanský palace where Bedřich Smetana lived and worked in 1863–1869

A wonderful view of Prague openes from the Seminary garden on the slope of the Petřín hill. In the centre are the two spires of the church of Our Lady beforeTýn. The closest tall church tower belongs to the Lesser Quarter White Friar church of Our Lady Victorious. With the valuable wax figure of the Prague Infant Jesus. Music in conection with architecture, visual art and the special charm of the city design made Prague a cultural jewel of Europe

In 1969 the international conference on the occasion of the 1100th anniversary of the death of the founder of the Slavonic spiritual culture Constantine took place in Prague. At the closing meeting of the participants to the symposium, the Czech-American linguist and Slavonic scholar Roman Jakobson had the toast. He knew Prague from its most intimate as well as the most beautiful aspects. Although living abroad for a long time he preserved love for the Czech land, its capital and its magnificent culture. In his toast, among other things, he said:

"I drink to the beauty by which I was gripped almost fifty years ago and which I had the occasion to remind and revive today. But it is not only the beauty of nature but also the great moral beauty of the people who live in this admirable country. – I myself sometimes wonder what is the reason that it is this country, the focal point of Europe where already in the time of Constantine the cultures of the East and the West met with its own cultural contribution, that has preserved at such a small area such a great number of great monuments of culture and gave the world such immense ideas as the idea of equality and sovereignty of all countries (Constantine), as the great ideas of Reformation (Huss) and that immense heritage of Comenius – democratization of knowledge. Well, let's take the Prague only! What is the reason that it is here that we find the vastest Romanesque monument of Europe – the Romanesque Strahov; that today in Prague there is the oldest Jewish synagogue in Europe; that Prague can boast of the oldest preserved complex of early Gothic buildings which is the St. Agnes's convent; that in Prague, in the district of Karlov there is the bravest Gothic vault in Europe; that in Prague within the green vegetation of gardens there is such a wonderful view of the most beautiful Renaissance edifice to the North of the Alps – the Royal Belvedere; that the most picturesque district of the city the Lesser Quarter is dominated by such a magnificent Baroque church with the biggest vault in Europe – St. Nicholas's cathedral. And in this city there is also the miracle of the 19th century – the National Theatre built from nothing with such love by the people for themselves. But there is yet something else which I appreciate most of all. None nation in the world that I've known has in itself such a great amount of democracy as the Czech people. It is a nation that has never in history oppressed any other nation. And if the country was governed by its domestic rulers even those who have been always and everywhere suppressed most of all – the Jews were not deprived of their dignity. The Czech land has become a home for me. I've understood the feelings of Antonín Dvořák when in a foreign country, over the ocean, he longed so much for his returning home to his homeland. I could hear in my mind that wonderful melody of his, that motif of home from his New World Symphony: Oh, my distant homeland... and now when I'm here, I can hear another music, that glorious closing of Smetana's Libuše since even though the mist is preventing me in clear vision I've lost nothing from those three virtues of Constantine's – love, faith and courage."

MILAN KUNA & JIŘÍ VŠETEČKA

PRAGUE IN HISTORY OF MUSIC

Cover, binding and typographical layout Václav Rytina
Translation into English by Daniel Hradilák
First edition, Prague 1997
Published by V RÁJI Publishing House (V Ráji 229, Prague 9),
64th edition, 176 pages, 156 colour photographs
Editors in chief Marie Vitochová and Jindřich Kejř
Printed by Východočeská tiskárna, spol. s r. o., Pardubice